THIS WORK WAS PUBLISHED BY
Red Flag Books
an imprint of Socialist Alternative

BROWSE HUNDREDS OF TITLES AT
shop.redflag.org.au

Published by Red Flag Books
Melbourne, May 2020

Red Flag Books is an imprint of Socialist Alternative
redflag.org.au

Cover design by Gene Brownlie
Interior layout by Chris Giddings
Edited by Annie Toller and Oscar Sterner

Printed by IngramSpark

The Story of Palestine: Empire, Repression and Resistance

VASHTI FOX

RED FLAG
BOOKS

Contents

1. Palestine Today — 9
2. The Birth of Israel — 21
   - A brief history of Zionism — 21
   - Zionism, imperialism and colonialism in the Middle East — 26
   - The Palestinian revolt — 30
3. Israel and Imperialism — 37
   - After 1948 — 38
   - The rising tide of nationalism — 40
   - 1967 and the "favoured regime" — 42
   - Subcontracting terror — 44
   - Israel and the Lebanese Civil War — 45
   - The War on Terror — 48
   - The 2006 Lebanon War — 50
   - Gaza 2009–10 — 52
   - Arab revolution and counter-revolution — 52
4. Oslo and Beyond: the Lie of Peace — 55
   - The origins of US "peace" — 55
   - Oslo — 56
   - 2003: The "Road Map to Peace" — 60
5. Australia and Israel — 63
   - Colonial settler states — 65
   - Australia, Israel and imperialism — 66
   - Australia: "Godparent of the Israeli state" — 67
   - An increasingly "special relationship" — 70
   - The 2006 Lebanon war — 71
   - Gaza — 72
   - Trade — 75
   - The myth of a "moral" Australian state — 76
   - The myth of the Zionist lobby — 78
   - Conclusion — 85

6. **Palestinian Resistance**   87
    Class dynamics in early Palestine   88
    The Palestine Communist Party   91
    Arab nationalism   93
    The PLO and Fatah   95
    Intifada   98
    The Fronts   101
    The Second Intifada   102
    Hamas   103
    The Arab Revolutions   106
    The Arab revolutions and Palestine   107

References   113

This book is a modest little contribution to the struggle for a better world. Like all good things it was a collective effort. In particular I would like to thank Sandra Bloodworth for her unswerving, passionate dedication to fight for a better world. She is a daily inspiration. Also, to Mick Armstrong for his unbounded enthusiasm for rebellion and his encyclopaedic knowledge of the revolutionary movement. To Omar Hassan, Tess Lee Ack and Sagar Sanyal for their political advice and their impeccable eye for detail. To Gene Brownlie for his gorgeous front cover design. To all the comrades globally, living and gone, who have struggled for a free Palestine. And finally, to my daughter Frankie, who I hope will live to see a planet worthy of her beautiful smile.

CHAPTER ONE

Palestine Today

> I heard you in the other room asking your mother, "Mama, am I a Palestinian?" When she answered "Yes" a heavy silence fell on the whole house. It was as if something hanging over our heads had fallen, its noise exploding, then – silence. Afterwards...I heard you crying. I could not move. There was something bigger than my awareness being born in the other room through your bewildered sobbing. It was as if a blessed scalpel was cutting up your chest and putting there the heart that belongs to you... I was unable to move to see what was happening in the other room. I knew, however, that a distant homeland was being born again: hills, olive groves, dead people, torn banners and folded ones, all cutting their way into a future of flesh and blood and being born in the heart of another child... Do you believe that man grows? No, he is born suddenly – a word, a moment, penetrates his heart to a new throb. One scene can hurl him down from the ceiling of childhood onto the ruggedness of the road.
>
> - Ghassan Kanafani[1]

To most of us, house keys are mundane objects: pieces of metal, plain and insignificant. But for tens of thousands of Palestinian refugees scattered across the Middle East, house keys – some rusty, some worn from constant touch – are cherished.

These keys serve no functional purpose because they are keys to lost homes, in villages and towns from which Palestinian families were driven in 1948 and 1967, some at gunpoint, some fleeing from fear of guns. They are keys to homes that are occupied by Israeli

---
1. Kanafani 1999.

strangers. They are keys to homes that were crushed by Israeli bulldozers, part of the Israeli state's program of ethnic cleansing.

These homeless keys represent for Palestinians the dream of a homeland, the right of return to their birthplace and the historic injustice committed against them.

Some of these keys were clutched tight during the Right of Return protests in the Gaza Strip which began in April 2018. During these mobilisations, many thousands of Palestinians marched on the heavily militarised zone between the Strip and Israel. They were attempting to draw attention to the plight of Palestinians living in the besieged city of over two million, where drinkable water, electricity, important medicines and many foodstuffs are scarce, while also attempting to redress the historic dispossession of their forebears.

A sense of desperation and determination echoes through the protesters' statements. "Some people believe we are idiots to think the Israelis will allow us in. They may not, but we will not stop trying to return", said one of the rally participants, Ahmed, a 37-year-old public servant and descendant of refugees from Jaffa. Another protester summed up a widespread sentiment: "No peace, no jobs, no unity and no future, so what difference would death make? If we are going to die, then let it not be in vain".[2]

William Faulkner said: "The past is not dead. It is not even past." Nowhere is this truer than Palestine. Historic and current injustice are ever present.

The history of Israel's brutality is often written on the bodies of Palestinians. Take Fadi Abu Silme, a 29-year-old father of two and husband of seven years. Silme grew up in Gaza, surviving the punitive siege on the territory and numerous Israeli bombings. Through the horror, he found love and made a family, but in 2008 an Israeli drone strike hit his home. He only just escaped with his life, but

---

2. SBS News, "The Great March of Return: Thousands of Palestinians charge border in protest", 14 April 2018.
https://www.sbs.com.au/news/the-great-march-of-return-thousands-of-palestinians-charge-border-in-protest.

had both legs amputated. Despite this injury, Silme participated in the March of Return. He went down daily to the protest camp in his wheelchair and hurled rocks into the dust and wind. He found humanity in this small act of rebellion. On 14 May he said goodbye to his children and wheeled himself off to the protest. He didn't return. He was shot by an Israeli sniper.

Silme was one of dozens of protesters killed that day, and one of thousands killed or wounded by Israeli weapons during the Great March of Return. The Israeli military said in a tweet of its approach: "Nothing was carried out uncontrolled; everything was accurate and measured and we know where every bullet landed."[3] The murder of over 110 unarmed Palestinians between 30 March and 15 May was deliberate, well planned and executed.

Death by Israel is a feature of life for Palestinians.

There are the deaths that appear quick and there are those that are slow. There are those that are dramatic and then there are those that occur in the quiet of the everyday. The three-week Israeli bombardment of Gaza from 27 December 2008 was an example of the former. In this offensive, also known as Operation Cast Lead, the Israeli military killed over 1,400 Gazans, the overwhelming majority of whom were civilians, 333 of whom were children.[4] War crimes, such as the use of the deadly chemical white phosphorus on civilian populations, were broadcast live across the world. A United Nations-commissioned investigation produced the Goldstone Report which revealed that Israeli military planners deliberately followed a doctrine which involved "the application of disproportionate force and the causing of great damage and destruction to civilian property and infrastructure, and suffering to civilian populations."[5] This was a big, bold declaration; Israel had the guns, the bombs and the chemicals, and they were prepared to use them on a largely defenceless, besieged population. Cast Lead was a declaration to

---

3. "Israeli Military Twitter", B'Tselem, 31 March 2018, https://twitter.com/btselem/status/980042213718708224.
4. Amnesty International UK 2017.
5. "Key points of the Goldstone Report", *Al Jazeera*, 3 October 2009. https://www.aljazeera.com/news/middleeast/2009/10/200910395820396287.html.

the world that Israel would kill Palestinians with an unabashed ruthlessness.

The 2014 bombardment echoed Cast Lead. Reports from the ground were just as distressing. A young man, a father of six, lying hysterical on the hospital floor declared to a television camera that he had just seen his children blown away "like paper in the wind". The Israeli army had just shelled a UN school that was meant to be a safe haven.[6] Another man described the anxiety, grief and tension of living in the densely populated coastal strip:

> Just imagine that moment when the Israeli army calls and orders you to evacuate your home to shell and destroy it within ten minutes.
>
> Imagine that! Just ten minutes and your little history will be wiped off the earth, your gifts and photos of your brothers and sons, the stuff you like: your chair, books...a letter from a migrant sister, memories of moments with whom you love, your habits of petting a gardenia on your window, your old clothes, your wife's gold and the money you saved over your life.
>
> Oh! Everything comes to your mind and astonishes you!
>
> And then, you took only your identification papers inside a candy tray and go out to die a thousand times or, instead, you stay and die for once.[7]

These are the dramatic deaths. There are many others.

Australian journalist John Pilger has described the everyday situation in Gaza as "creeping genocide".[8] This is the perfect description for the routine violence that Israel enacts on the Palestinian population. This is the violence that rarely elicits global headlines, violence that is all the more shocking for the silence that surrounds it.

The Gaza Strip is suffering an Israeli-imposed economic blockade that is slowly killing its 2.5 million inhabitants. Between 2007 and 2010, Israeli authorities devised mathematical formulae to determine how much food to allow into the Strip, based on a count

---

6. Ben Hubbard and Jodi Rudoren, "Israel Shelled UN school killing 20 Palestinians fleeing violence says relief agency", *Sydney Morning Herald*, 31 July 2014.
7. Alray, "Aggressive war", 10 July 2004.
   https://alray.ps/en/index.php?act=post&id=5039#.XpaWYsgzbIU.
8. John Pilger, "Palestine Is Still the Issue" (a Carlton Television production for ITV, 2002). http://johnpilger.com/videos/palestine-is-still-the-issue.

of how many calories were needed to allow the population to only just survive.

The siege of Gaza results in the Strip having only four hours of electricity a day. Running essential services is extremely difficult. Gaza's hospitals rely on generators that often fail. Death rates in hospitals are high. Ninety-seven percent of Gaza's drinking water is contaminated. Sara Roy from Harvard's Centre for Middle Eastern Studies said in 2018: "Innocent people, most of them young, are slowly being poisoned by the water they drink".[9] According to the World Bank, unemployment levels in Gaza are some of the highest in the world. As of October 2019 unemployment sits at 60 percent for people aged between 15 and 29.[10] After regular bombings, in 2008–09 and then again in 2014, buildings turned to rubble. Israel has banned important construction materials so many of these buildings remain hollow, bombed-out shells.

Palestinian political freedoms are limited in Gaza. Indeed, the initial impetus behind the 2008–09 bombing was the fact that Gazans voted democratically to elect a party, Hamas, that the Israelis disapproved of.

Life in the occupied West Bank is only marginally better. The apartheid wall, described by African American novelist Alice Walker "an insult to the soul of humanity,"[11] continues to snake through Palestinian communities, dividing them and stealing their land. This wall is twice as high and three times as long as the Berlin Wall, and is a constant visual reminder to the Palestinians that they do not control their own territory, that they are monitored 24 hours a day.

Palestinian land and homes are regularly bulldozed and stolen by an aggressive Israeli settler movement, backed up and endorsed by the Israeli state. There are, as of June 2019, 132 official settlements in the West Bank, 11 settlements in East Jerusalem and around 113 outposts or unofficial settlements. Outposts are often clustered around the official settlements and over time become more fixed

---

9. Finkelstein 2018.
10. The World Bank 2019.
11. Abunimah 2011.

and permanent. Both are methods of land theft and they operate in tandem. According to the European Union, approximately 630,000 official Israeli settlers live in the West Bank and East Jerusalem.[12] These figures have surged under the leadership of Benjamin Netanyahu, and there was a marked rise in approval of settlements after the election of Donald Trump in the US.

The arrival of the settlers in Palestinian areas is regularly accompanied by violence against individuals and property. One report recorded 10,672 olive trees vandalised by settlers in 2013 alone, and 9,390 in 2014. The olive-oil industry in the Occupied Territories accounts for 25 percent of agricultural income of the West Bank and supports approximately 100,000 families.[13] Palestinians are mercilessly hounded by Israeli settlers attempting to gain access to more land. Attacks are regular. They involve bashings, shootings, arson, verbal and physical intimidation. In 2014 alone, the United Nations Office for the Coordination of Humanitarian Affairs recorded 324 incidents targeting Palestinians. They argue that the nature of the attacks has become more vicious and more frequent.[14]

One Palestinian family from the West Bank village of Burin, which is a few hundred metres from the outpost of Arosa, describes how settlers regularly patrol near their village with guns, often accompanied by Israeli soldiers. In December of 2010 settlers "hurled a cocktail bomb on the house while the family was sleeping. The bomb hit and burned the window of the room where the kids were sleeping".[15] The children were saved, but this kind of regular harassment leaves a deep psychological legacy.

These settlements have displaced thousands of Palestinians, ripping them from their property and homes. They have also undermined the contiguity of Palestinian territory, making self-determination all but impossible. New laws are regularly introduced into the Israeli parliament, or Knesset, that codify these settlements,

---

12. European Union 2019.
13. Ayoub 2016.
14. United Nations 2018.
15. Ayoub 2016.

bringing more Palestinian land under Israeli legal control. This is what twenty-first century colonisation looks like.

Palestinian life in the West Bank is punctuated by other daily indignities. To get to work, visit family or go shopping, many thousands of Palestinians are forced to walk through armed checkpoints. These checkpoints resemble cages and are opened or shut at seemingly random intervals. So Palestinians are made to wait, held at gunpoint, sometimes for hours, before they can get to their destination. Edward Said described the situation in 2002 and things have not changed since:

> There is the waiting in the sun for hours; then there is the detention of medical supplies and produce until they rot; there are the insulting words and beatings administered at will; the sudden rampage of jeeps and soldiers against civilians waiting their turn by the thousands at the innumerable check points that have made Palestinian life a choking hell; making dozens of youths kneel in the sun for hours; forcing men to take off their clothes; insulting and humiliating parents in front of their children; forbidding the sick to pass through for no other reason than personal whim; stopping ambulances and firing on them.[16]

Many comparisons have been drawn with apartheid South Africa. Palestinian writer Linah Alsaafin said: "Apartheid is very much alive in occupied Palestine. It is our reality that we breathe through our congested lungs every minute of our waking lives."[17]

Leaders of the South African anti-apartheid movement, such as Archbishop Desmond Tutu, have drawn similar conclusions:

> I visited the Occupied Palestinian Territories, and have witnessed the humiliation of Palestinians at Israeli military checkpoints. The inhumanity that won't let ambulances reach the injured, farmers tend their land, or children attend schools. This treatment is familiar to me as it was to many Black South Africans who were corralled and harassed by the security forces of the apartheid government.[18]

Just like Black South Africans, the Palestinian population is

---

16. Said 2003.
17. Alsaafin 2011.
18. Barrows-Friedman 2011.

criminalised and imprisoned at disproportionately high rates. In 1967 the Israeli military forcibly occupied the West Bank and Gaza. Since then more than 800,000 Palestinians have been arrested. Around 40 percent of male Palestinians in the occupied territories have been arrested at least once.

Political expression by Palestinians living in the West Bank is criminalised. Palestinian protesters are regularly arrested and detained. The number of Palestinian political prisoners is high. As of January 2020 Israel held 5,000 political prisoners, 180 of whom were children. Out of these 431 were administrative detainees: prisoners who are arrested and held indefinitely without charge or trial.[19] All information about administrative detainees is secret. These practices echo the worst years of the most brutal colonial regimes.

Ideologues for the Israeli state make much of its democratic nature, but commitment to formal parliamentary democracy is brittle. For the Israeli ruling class, maintaining a Jewish majority is vital. Political dominance flows from numerical dominance. According to Israel's Central Bureau of Statistics, there are 542,000 Jews and 324,000 Palestinians living in East Jerusalem. Data from the Israeli water corporation indicates, however, that there are tens of thousands of Palestinians who have been left out of these statistics. If they were taken into account, the Jewish majority would contract to 59 percent.[20] These statistics are of great concern to the Israeli Jewish majority, whose artificially constructed and brutally enforced demographic dominance in Israel allows them to maintain the fiction of democracy.

Israel claims to be one of the most fair and progressive countries in the region. In reality it is a religious ethno-state in which the non-Jewish population experiences systematic discrimination. Palestinians living inside the 1948 borders of Israel suffer from

---

19. Addameer: Prisoner support and human rights association, *Prisoner statistics: January 2020*. http://www.addameer.org/statistics.
20. Nir Hason, "Experts: Tens of thousands of Palestinians living in East Jerusalem unaccounted for in data", *Haaretz*, 17 May 2017.
https://www.haaretz.com/israel-news/premium-experts-tens-of-thousands-of-extra-palestinians-living-in-east-jerusalem-1.5473112.

formal and informal, institutional and structural oppression. Over half the Arab population within Israel lives under the poverty line. Unemployment rates remain consistently higher among the Arab population. A study by the Adalah Centre in Israel found that:

> Palestinian citizens of Israel often face discrimination in work opportunities, pay and conditions, both because of the inadequate implementation of equal-opportunity legislation and because of entrenched structural barriers, which particularly affect women, and include poor or non-existent public transportation, a lack of industrial zones, and a shortage of state-run day-care centres. Palestinian citizens are also excluded from the labor force by the use of the military-service criterion as a condition for acceptance for employment, often when there is no connection between the nature of the work and military experience.[21]

There are around 65 laws that explicitly discriminate against the Palestinians living in Israel. More than half of these laws were introduced since 2000. The last decade has seen legal victories for the far right in Israeli politics. Avigdor Lieberman, the leader of the ultra-nationalist Yisrael Beiteinu party, pushed through a loyalty oath bill in 2010 which mandated that new non-Jewish citizens swear allegiance to Israel as a "Jewish democratic state". Ahmed Tibi, an Israeli-Arab member of the Knesset, condemned the cabinet's decision at the time: "The government of Israel has become subservient to Yisrael Beiteinu [Lieberman's party] and its fascist doctrine," he said. "No other state in the world would force its citizens or those seeking citizenship to pledge allegiance to an ideology."[22] In 2018 a new law was passed that removes Israeli citizenship from Palestinians living in Jerusalem who breach "loyalty to Israel".[23] Such loyalty is a nebulous concept that can mean

---

21. Adalah – The Legal Center for Arab Minority Rights in Israel, *The Inequality Report*, March 2011.
https://www.adalah.org/uploads/oldfiles/upfiles/2011/Adalah_The_Inequality_Report_March_2011.pdf.2011
22. Harriet Sherwood, "Israel proposes Jewish state loyalty oath for new citizens", *The Guardian*, 11 October 2010.
https://www.theguardian.com/world/2010/oct/10/israel-jewish-oath-new-citizens.
23. "Israel passes law to strip residency from Jerusalem Palestinians," *Al Jazeera*, 8 March 2018.
https://www.aljazeera.com/news/2018/03/israel-passes-law-strip-residency-jerusalem-palestinians-180307153033538.html.

membership of a Palestinian party or sympathies with states that Israel considers enemies. This move accompanied the much publicised shifting of the US embassy in Israel from Tel Aviv to Jerusalem, a provocative declaration that the US administration, under Trump, backs Israel's attempts to colonise all of Jerusalem and claim it as its undivided capital.

The shift to the right in official Israeli politics has engendered increasing levels of hostility to Palestinians among Jewish Israelis. In 2015, a Pew study found that 48 percent of all Israeli Jews agree with the statement: "Arabs should be expelled or transferred from Israel."[24] In any other context this would be called ethnic cleansing. A poll conducted by Haifa University revealed worsening attitudes of Jewish citizens of Israel towards Arabs or Palestinians. The number of respondents who recognise the right of Arabs to live in the country as a minority with full citizens' rights declined from 79.7 percent in 2015 to 73.8 percent in 2018. The number of Jews willing to have Arab pupils in their schools dropped from 57.5 percent to 51.6 percent and those refusing to have Arab neighbours rose from 41 percent to 48 percent.[25]

These trends in both formal policy and popular racism towards Arabs and Palestinians are reflective of the deep and structural racism of the Israeli state. Since the beginning of Zionist colonisation there has been an attempt by Israelis and their supporters to deny Palestinians not just their land, but their very existence. In a move similar to the declaration of *terra nullius* in Australia, the Zionist movement declared Palestine ideal for Zionist migration as it was "a land without a people for a people without a land". This process has not ended.

The picture across Gaza, the West Bank and inside the 1948 borders of Israel is one of increasing Israeli brutality, control and

---

24. Ben Sales, "Pew: 48 percent of Israeli Jews want Arabs out of the country", *Jewish Telegraph Agency*, 8 March 2016.
https://www.jta.org/2016/03/08/israel/six-surprising-findings-from-pews-study-of-israelis.
25. Ben Lynefield, "Israel's Jews and Arab minority further apart than ever, says poll", *The National*, 10 March 2018.
https://www.thenational.ae/world/israel-s-jews-and-arab-minority-further-apart-than-ever-poll-says-1.711840.

colonial expansion. Violence, the everyday and the sensational, is part and parcel of the Israeli state. The rest of this pamphlet will address why and how this all happened and why and how Israel continues to receive strong support from all major Western states. The story is not simply one of Palestinian victimhood, however. Since before the establishment of the Israeli state, the Palestinians have resisted. They have fought bravely and against the odds. The last chapter of this pamphlet will explore the history and the politics of the Palestinian resistance movement and make an argument about the kinds of resistance required to win liberation.

CHAPTER TWO

The Birth of Israel

Propagandists for the Israeli state like to pretend that Israel always was, and therefore will always be. Contrary to such myths, Israel came into being due to a very specific conjuncture of events. Namely, the coming together of the requirements of British imperialism to dominate an oil-rich part of the world with a movement that could serve its interests, Zionism. This chapter will sweep aside the ideological detritus and tell the story of Zionism and its relationship to the British empire and global imperialism.

A brief history of Zionism

The undeniable horrors of the Holocaust are routinely used to justify the establishment of the state of Israel. In fact, Zionism, and the desire to establish a Jewish-only state, existed long before the unprecedented barbarity of the Nazi concentration camps. Zionism emerged as a movement in the late 1880s in Eastern Europe and Russia. It was primarily a political, rather than a religious movement, which saw an exclusive Jewish state as the solution to the marginalisation, economic oppression and discrimination experienced by Jews. The goal was to establish a Jewish-only homeland, which would give the aspiring Zionist leaders their own state to rule, their own place to be powerful. Multiple sites were initially considered, in places as diverse as Uganda, Japan and Australia, but eventually Palestine became the preferred site. Immigration to Palestine by small groups of Zionists began in the 1890s.

Marxist historian Abram Leon described the initial impetus of Zionism thus:

> From its inception, Zionism appeared as a reaction of the Jewish petty bourgeoisie, hard hit by the mounting anti-Semitic wave, kicked from one country to another, and striving to attain the Promised Land where it might find shelter from the tempests sweeping the modern world.[1]

This reaction to an essentially modern convergence of phenomena and events (the development of capitalism, increasing nationalism, anti-Semitic pogroms) was presented as an age-old, eternal philosophy. Much like other nationalisms, Zionism developed a lengthy historical imaginary. Zionism claimed for itself the historic desires of world Jewry; a 2000-year-old quest for the settlement of Jews in their own state in Palestine. This mythology, argues Leon, reads back into history a desire that was never there: "The Jewish tavern owner or 'farmer' of sixteenth-century Poland thought as little of 'returning' to Palestine as does the Jewish millionaire in America today".[2]

Zionism was a minority current in Jewish populations across the world. The migration data tells part of the story. Estimates suggest three million Eastern European Jews went to the USA and half a million to Western Europe between 1880 and 1920. These figures vastly overwhelm the 120,000 Jews who went to Palestine by 1930.[3] If there was a promised land that dominated Jewish imagination, it was America.

Furthermore, attitudes to Zionism were often shaped by class. The vast majority of working-class Jews did not hold to the notion of a Jewish nation. They were socially embedded in their home countries. To the extent these Jews were organised, they were

1. Leon 1950.
2. ibid.
3. Rose 1986, p27.

mostly members of socialist organisations and saw their project as fighting for equality and self-emancipation in their home countries. For instance, in Poland it is estimated that in seven major cities with a total Jewish population of about 840,000, some 40 percent voted for the Bund, the Yiddish socialist organisation.[4] For many of the millions of Jewish working-class supporters of socialism, Zionist ideas were anathema, a retreat from the struggle for justice in the places they lived.

Yosef Goldshtain, a historian of Jewish civilization, argues that:

> In sum, Zionism attracted the middle-class Jews who were open to new tendencies but sought to maintain Jewish tradition. The intelligentsia and the working class...did not join the movement in its early days, despite the fact that the leadership came from the intelligentsia. The Jewish proletariat was not attracted to the Zionist movement because the latter offered it no immediate social, economic and cultural solutions. A major portion of the Jewish proletariat was drawn to the Bund and the Jewish intellectual sought more to be integrated into the surrounding society than to join the Zionist movement.[5]

Indeed, the Zionist leadership was conscious of the fact that its main ideological enemies in the Jewish population were the socialist Bund. Zionist leader Chaim Weizmann said in 1903: "Our hardest struggle everywhere is against the Bund...this movement consumes much energy and heroism...children are in open revolt against their parents".[6] Heated debates were held in towns between the two forces. Future Israeli prime minister David Ben-Gurion's biographer describes an example in 1905 in the Polish town of Plonsk. The debate took place in the town's Great Synagogue. The Bund sent one of its best speakers, shops were closed and "out of respect for the synagogue...handguns were placed on the table".[7]

The defeat of the 1905 revolution in Russia and the associated repression across Europe began to push back the revolutionary movement generally and the Bund specifically. The strength of

---
4. Gitelman 2003, p8.
5. ibid., p16.
6. Rose 2004, p106.
7. ibid., p111.

socialist ideas inside the Jewish working class of Eastern Europe meant, however, that some Zionist currents were forced to try and incorporate Marxist ideas into Zionism or fear total marginalisation. While many Jews joined socialist organisations, such as the Bolsheviks or Mensheviks, others began to be drawn toward Zionism. A plethora of socialist Zionist or labour Zionist groups emerged. These groups attempted to appeal to Jewish workers on the basis that Palestine could be transformed into a socialist country through Zionist immigration and the creation of a Jewish proletariat. Arabs barely appeared in the rhetoric.

Socialist Zionist groups, such as Poale Zion, theorised this notion by attempting to incorporate nationalism into the class struggle.[8] This was an uneasy mix. Poale Zion and the other dominant labour Zionist groups, including their peak body in Israel, the Jewish trade union called the Histadrut, emphasised the importance of "Hebrew" or Jewish labour as the basis for the new state.[9] In practice this meant two things. Firstly, it meant actively discouraging Jewish businesses from employing Arab or Palestinian workers. This involved picketing, boycotts or physically attacking businesses that employed Arabs. Secondly, it meant refusing to organise Arab or Palestinian workers, or, when they did go on strike, actively undermining their actions.[10] Indeed, the Histadrut refused to allow Arab workers to join. The Histadrut was not simply a traditional union. It was also a major employer, one of the largest in British-mandate Palestine. This had the effect of turning Marxist ideas of solidarity and internationalism on their head. John Rose puts it succinctly: "These 'principles' of the Jewish trade union movement in Palestine anticipated the foundations of the Israeli state itself: the institutionalised separation of Arab and Jew, privileging the Jew at the expense of the Arab".[11] In other words; this was apartheid.

---

8. Borochov 1906.
9. A minority left current split away to form Left Poale Zion in 1919–1920. This group attempted to stem the reactionary nationalist tide and organised both Arab and Palestinian workers.
10. Beinin 1990, p48.
11. Rose 2004, p113.

The initial marginality of Zionist ideas among Europe's Jewish population in the early twentieth century demonstrates that Zionism was a political current that had to be fought for. It was not a "natural" reflection of an eternal Jewish desire for a homeland in Palestine. This was a notion that was created and fostered by Zionist ideologues.

While working-class Jews were overwhelmingly uninterested in Zionism until after 1905, Jews who had become part of the establishment, particularly in Western Europe, were more sympathetic. This sympathy stemmed from two places. Firstly, many were concerned that the forced displacement of poorer Jews within Eastern Europe would further inflame anti-Semitism and affect the advancement and security of wealthier Jews as rulers and non-Jewish populations reacted against the inflows of migrants. Zionism therefore seemed like an attractive prospect for this class of Jewish people, as it promised to encourage emigration of the poorer Jewish population out of Europe altogether. Secondly, wealthier Jews developed aspirations for a state of their own, one where they could make their fortune without limitation or restriction. These wealthy Jews would, over time, become more committed to the Zionist project and provide an economic base for the immigration programs.

The Zionist movement was so committed to the project of establishing a Jewish population in Palestine that it opposed any forces that might encourage Jewish migration elsewhere. Indeed, throughout the Second World War and the Holocaust, Zionist leaders such as Ben-Gurion refused to push for Western countries such as England, the USA and Australia to accept Jewish refugees.

Speaking in December 1938, Ben-Gurion, "[r]ather than see all the children escape safely to England...argued that it was better to let half of them be slaughtered at the hands of the Nazis in order to get the surviving half to be settlers in his colonial project".[12] Indeed one of the leaders of the Irgun, an underground Zionist paramilitary force, met Nazi Adolf Eichmann in Berlin

---

12. Suarez 2017, p57.

and claimed he would exchange information on the Allied forces for a promise that the Nazis would send Jewish emigrants to Palestine only.[13]

The Zionist exclusivist project, based on an interpretation of history that says Jews and gentiles can never live together amicably, inevitably tends toward racial and ethnic separatism, unholy alliances and racism. For instance the Jewish Agency, the peak Zionist body in Palestine before 1929, had a constitution which included phrases like Jewish "purity of blood"[14] and mandated that Jews and non-Jews should not be allowed to marry.

Zionism, imperialism and colonialism in the Middle East

Having initially neither guns, diplomatic clout nor a state to pursue their interests, the Zionists needed to appeal to the imperial powers to aid them in their project. They met with representatives of the Russian, German, French and British states. The British were the most open to their proposals, seeing the advantage in building up a colonial population of mainly European Jews in the strategic zone of Palestine. These interests converged with those of the Zionists. Theodor Herzl, for instance, described the role the Jewish state would play in Palestine as a "portion of the rampart of Europe against Asia, an outpost of civilisation as opposed to barbarism".[15] Even more explicit was Max Nordau, the co-founder of the World Zionist Organisation, who delivered a speech in 1920 to a variety of British officials in London.

> We considered your views and were loyal toward your proposals. We only want to continue. We made a pact with you. We consider carefully the dangers and commitments of this pact. We know what you hope to receive from us. We must protect the Suez Canal for you. We shall be the guards of your road to India as it passes through the Middle East. We are ready to fulfil this difficult military role but this requires that you

---

13. ibid., p99.
14. ibid., p66.
15. Quoted in Gitelman 2003, p16.

permit us to become powerful so as to be able to fulfil our role. Loyalty for loyalty, faithfulness in return for faithfulness.[16]

As European capitalism expanded in the latter part of the nineteenth century, the major European powers began to scramble for control of the rest of the world. They ransacked entire continents for their resources, enslaved their populations and created enclaves of dominance. Imperialism impelled the ruling classes of the European nations into increasing competition with each other. Old empires had to crumble as new ones were forged.

The Middle East became central to this process. Even before oil became such a significant commodity, the region was a vital bridge for trade between Western Europe and Asia. Control over these trading routes was vital to all the European powers and the Ottoman empire, and when diplomatic skirmishes couldn't solve the inevitable impasses, military conflicts ensued.

World War One broke out as a natural result of the competition between the major capitalist powers over control of the world. The war was essentially about redrawing the global map into spheres of influence and control. In some instances, this redrawing was literal. At a meeting of the British cabinet in December 1915, the government's chief adviser on the Middle East, Colonel Sir Mark Sykes, said: "I should like to draw a line from the 'e' in Acre to the last 'k' in Kirkuk", as he stooped, finger poised, over a map of the Middle East.[17] The discussion was a prelude to a secret agreement between the French and the British about how the Middle East should be divided. The Sykes-Picot Agreement, as it became known, set the contours of the next century's imperial battles.

The agreement, signed in May 1916, and finessed over the subsequent nine years, formed the modern Middle East out of the detritus of the Ottoman empire. Parts of Syria and what is now known as Lebanon would come under French control, while Britain would take southern and central Mesopotamia (Iraq) and Palestine.

---

16. Honig-Parnass and Haddad (eds) 2007, "Introduction".
17. Cited in Barr 2011, p12.

While Palestine itself was of little direct economic interest, it was important for the defence of British positions in Egypt. The great powers negotiated that it would have an international administration, while the rest of Syria, northern Iraq and Jordan would have nominal Arab leaderships. In reality these leaderships would be working under the auspices of the British and French, in the south and north respectively.

Sykes-Picot created countries and borders where there had been none, establishing imperial domination and fostering divisions amongst the indigenous populations of the region that still bear upon these peoples today. A British finger tracing a line across a map literally shaped the lives and fates of millions of people yet to be born.

Even within the power blocs that formed during the war there were tensions and rivalries. James Barr, author of *A Line in the Sand* said, "No sooner than Sykes and Georges Picot had cooked up this deal the British started thinking about how they might get around it."[18] Karl Marx describes the ruling class as a "band of warring brothers", and so it was: Britain and France were allies by day but competitors by night. While Britain was negotiating with the French over the division of the Middle East, it was simultaneously negotiating with various Arab dynasties in the person of Hussein bin Ali, Sharif of Mecca, a self-appointed representative of various Arab nationalities. Hussein was prepared to lead a force against the Ottomans in exchange for the promise of a substantial kingdom after the war. While these promises were being made, the British were also negotiating with the Zionist movement.

British support for Jewish migration to Palestine and for a Jewish homeland was part of the project of establishing sympathetic communities in the Middle East that could be relied upon to back the British imperialist project. In 1917 the British signed the Balfour Declaration, a statement of its support for the establishment of a Jewish state in Palestine. In October 1918 Leo Amery, a

---

18. Cited in Quince 2016.

key member of prime minister Lloyd George's secretariat, argued that "strategically Palestine and Egypt go together". Palestine was "a necessary buffer to the Suez Canal" and "geographically practically the centre of the British Empire".[19] Winston Churchill advocated for the Balfour Declaration. In an article entitled "Zionism versus Bolshevism", published in 1920, he made clear the rationale: "[A] Jewish state under the protection of the British Crown, which might comprise three or four million Jews...would from every point of view be beneficial and would be especially in harmony with the truest interests of the British Empire".[20]

Under Britain's protective wing, the Zionist project advanced considerably. In 1882 there were 24,000 Jews in Palestine, many of whom were not Zionists and were an integrated part of the broader population; by 1914 there were 85,000. Another wave of immigration between 1919 and 1923 brought a further 85,000. Such high levels of immigration, either directly sponsored or tacitly endorsed by the British, were bound to bring about conflict with the other inhabitants of the area, the Palestinians. The first serious clashes under the mandate took place in April 1920, when serious rioting in Jerusalem left five Jews and four Arabs dead.

Britain was awarded control over Palestine by the League of Nations in 1922. The fate of the Palestinians had been wrenched from their hands; their future would now be determined in the remote diplomatic circles of Europe.

British support for the Zionists had to be balanced with the relationships the British had built up with various Arab rulers. One solution to this imperial conundrum was to partition Palestine, give the Zionists their own state, crush Palestinian hostility and hope Arab rulers would accept a new status quo. Various plans for the partition of historic Palestine were developed, put forward and rejected by one or another party as unfair and biased.

The Zionists were concerned that too many promises had been

---

19. Newsinger 2006, p122.
20. Rose 1986, p32.

made to the Arabs and that the British wouldn't follow through on their deal, while many Arabs were enraged by what they saw as the British and French betrayal. These endless negotiations and betrayals set the scene for the fiery nationalist movements of subsequent decades. "[Colonial rule] was not well received by the peoples of this region, and where they were able to rise up they did", says historian Rashid Khalidi.[21]

The Palestinian revolt

In 1936 there was an immense Palestinian uprising against British occupation and Zionist immigration. Tensions had been fuelled by dispossession, social and political exclusion, and violent repression of the Palestinian population. In such a context young Palestinians were inspired by reading about the broader ferment in Egypt and Syria and began joining nationalist clubs in the major cities. Rising unemployment among both Jews and Arabs across Palestine added to the heated atmosphere and tensions between these populations.

This revolt was one of the most significant in the history of the Arab world. It lasted for three years and involved a general strike of 175 days. It evolved into a guerrilla war that eventually left 37 British troops and police, 80 Zionist settlers, and more than a thousand Palestinians dead. The British only regained control of the situation through sheer terror. Villages were bombed, thousands of Palestinians were interned without trial, harsh collective punishments were imposed, routine use was made of Arab hostages as human shields, and ID cards were introduced. Between 1938 and 1939 at least one Arab was sentenced to death every week.

A British doctor named Elliot Forster documented in his diary an operation in Halhoul, a village near Hebron, in May 1939. Villagers had been herded into open-air pens, one for men and one for women, during a heat wave, and deprived of food and drink. The women were allowed to leave the pen after two days, but many of the men were kept for much longer and at least 10 died. Forster concluded

---

21. Quince 2016.

that the British could probably teach Hitler a thing or two about running concentration camps.[22]

The Palestinian movement was severely diminished by the end of the revolt. The brutality of the British meant that the Zionists emerged out of the conflict stronger. Indeed, some of the Zionist paramilitaries had used the revolt as an opportunity to practise their military manoeuvres. One of these, the Haganah, had units that were attached to British forces and in one instance in 1938 jointly attacked and then occupied a Palestinian village near what is now Israel. By the end of the revolt the Zionists were ready to consolidate their strength on the ground.

At the same time, the looming prospect of another war in Europe meant the British empire was keen to retain Arab loyalty. Some concessions were therefore made to the Palestinians: in 1939 the British government issued a white paper that limited Jewish migration to 75,000 a year. This move outraged the Zionist movement, which began more aggressively pursuing an argument for the development of an independent Zionist state. Throughout the war this involved developing political, economic and military power.

This economic power was facilitated by a variety of bodies; chief among them was the Jewish National Fund (JNF). The JNF was the body that purchased Palestinian land for the Zionist population more generally. From the onset it was designed to become "the 'custodian', on behalf of the Jewish people".[23]

By the end of the mandate in 1948, the Jewish community formally owned around 5.8 percent of the land in Palestine. These purchases would result in the expulsion of Palestinian peasants from the land they had worked for generations. They would be replaced with Jewish labour. Yet the JNF was not content with minority land ownership. According to Israeli historian Ilan Pappé, the JNF and its associates began to forensically map Palestinian villages:

> Precise details were recorded about the topographic location of each

---
22. Rose 2004, p131.
23. Pappé 2008, p17.

village, its access roads, quality of land, water springs, main sources of income, its socio-political composition, religious affiliations, names of its *muhktars* [leaders], its relationship with other villages, the age of individual men (16 to 50) and many more. An important category was an index of "hostility" (towards the Zionist project, that is), decided by the level of the village's participation in the revolt of 1936. There was a list of everyone who had been involved in the revolt and the families of those who had lost someone in the fight against the British.[24]

This mapping of the Palestinian villages and populations was designed to build up Zionist information that would enable their military commands to organise their offensive in 1948.

Accompanying land purchasing and this strategic mapping was the build-up of a range of Zionist paramilitary and military forces. Three of the most famous were the Irgun (Etzel), the Haganah and the Stern Gang (Lehi): all terrorists in today's terminology. The Haganah was formed in 1920, initially as a body designed to "defend" Jewish communities in Palestine. It became the official military wing of the Jewish Agency, which was the peak Zionist governing body at the time. It worked alongside the British throughout the 1920s and the Second World War. On the extreme edge, but working in tandem with the Haganah, were the Irgun and the Stern Gang. The Irgun was a more militant split from the Haganah and the Stern Gang a split from the Irgun. Together all three forces were well stocked militarily, and by 1947 posed a formidable military threat.

The development of such military and economic power was part of the goal of establishing a Jewish-only state. For Zionist leaders such as Ben-Gurion an exclusive Jewish state was the goal, the ethnic cleansing of Palestine was the means. He stated in 1947 to senior members of the Mapai party:

> There are 40 per cent non-Jews in the areas allocated to the Jewish state. The composition is not a solid basis for a Jewish state. And we have to face this new reality with all its severity and distinctness. Such a demographic

---

24. ibid., p19.

balance questions our ability to maintain Jewish sovereignty... Only a state with at least 80 per cent Jew is a viable and stable state.[25]

The Palestinians could become an internal threat, a fifth column, so "better to expel them", he said.[26] The establishment of Israel depended on the ethnic cleansing of the indigenous Arab population.

The end of World War Two transformed the global configurations of power. The USSR and the United States emerged as the two dominant economic and military behemoths. Their evolving antagonism would come to shape politics across the globe in the post-war period. Simultaneously, British power was declining, and direct rule over its massive colonial empire was becoming increasingly difficult to maintain. Faced with insurgent anti-colonial movements in country after country, it began to withdraw.

Britain turned to the UN to enact a succession plan which was to involve dividing Palestine into two states: one for the Zionists and the other for the Palestinians, with Jerusalem as an international city. In late November 1947, a plan was largely agreed upon by the UN General Assembly. The Jewish state was given 56 percent of the land; the city of Jaffa was included as an enclave of the Arab state; and the land known today as the Gaza Strip was split from its surrounding agricultural regions. This proposal left everyone unhappy. Even the CIA knew that the Zionists would never be happy with the proposed settlement. They wrote, in a secret report on 28 November 1947, the day before the UN passed the partition resolution, that:

> In the long run no Zionists in Palestine will be satisfied with the territorial arrangements of the partition settlement. [They] will continue to wage a strong propaganda campaign in the US and in Europe [and] the demand for more territory will be made as Jewish immigration floods the Jewish sector.[27]

Meanwhile, the Zionist militias and terrorist groups launched armed offensives against British targets and terrorised local Palestinians.

---

25. ibid., p48.
26. ibid., p49.
27. Suarez 2017, p173.

The Zionists wanted to establish "facts on the ground" that could force a more favourable UN settlement. In order to hasten British departure, the Irgun bombed a series of British targets. The most famous of these was the 1946 attack on the King David Hotel, the site of the central British mandate offices in Palestine. Ninety-one people were killed.

These attacks on the British were overshadowed, however, by the offensive against the local Palestinian population. Ilan Pappé's detailed research has revealed that the final plan for Zionist colonisation of Palestinian territory in 1948 involved mass expulsions, using tactics that included:

> Large-scale intimidation; laying siege to and bombarding villages and population centres; setting fire to homes, properties, and goods; expulsion; demolition; and, finally, planting mines among the rubble to prevent any of the expelled inhabitants from returning.[28]

In short, the plan was "an initiative to ethnically cleanse the country as a whole".[29] This was a plan driven by the Zionist leadership. Ben-Gurion himself, writing to his son in 1937, appeared convinced that ethnic cleansing was the only course of action open to Zionism: "The Arabs will have to go".[30] Such callous attitudes led to massacres. One of the most well known of these was in the Palestinian village of Deir Yassin. Members of the Irgun killed many in the village. Jacques de Reynier, an eyewitness from the International Red Cross, describes arriving in the village and seeing the scene:

> Here the "cleaning up" had been done with machine guns, then hand grenades. It had been finished off with knives, anyone could see that... I heard something like a sigh. I looked everywhere, turned over all the bodies and eventually found a little foot, still warm. It was a little girl of 10, mutilated by a hand grenade, but still alive...everywhere it was the same horrible sight...there had been 400 people in this village. About 50 of them had escaped and were still alive. All the rest

---
28. Pappé 2006.
29. ibid.
30. Pappé 2008, p23.

had been deliberately massacred in cold blood for, as I observed for myself, this gang [the Irgun] were admirably disciplined and only acted under orders.[31]

Zionist historians and Israeli politicians have tried to present the massacre at Deir Yassin as merely an act of youthful excess or the work of dissident terrorists. The truth is that the Irgun's actions were deliberate and politically motivated. This is revealed by their press statement released after the attack: "We intend to attack, conquer and keep until we have the whole of Palestine and Transjordan in a Greater Jewish State. This attack is the first step."[32] Though mainstream Zionist leaders formally distanced themselves from the violence, the Irgun was a short time later integrated into the Haganah and many of its leaders promoted. One of the Irgun leaders, Menachim Begin, eventually became Israeli prime minister in 1977.

After Deir Yassin, Zionists used violence or the threat of violence to compel Palestinians to flee. At least 70 massacres occurred, and around 13,000 Palestinians were killed. Sometimes, parents were killed while their children were forced to watch. Others were spared, but told that if they wanted to live, they should leave immediately. Five hundred and thirty Palestinian villages were razed. There are small stories of casual violence. Audeh Rantisi, tells of his family's expulsion from the town of al-Lydd in July 1948:

> Outside the gate, the soldiers stopped us and ordered everyone to throw all valuables onto a blanket. One young man and his wife of six weeks, friends of our family, stood near me. He refused to give up his money. Almost casually, the soldier pulled up his rifle and shot the man. He fell, bleeding and dying while his bride screamed and cried. I felt nauseated and sick, my whole body numbed by shock waves.[33]

Others tell of the offensive from the skies. "They bombed us from the air just as we were breaking the fast for Ramadan – they knew we would all be in our homes," said the poet Taha Muhammad Ali. He and his family fled the town after the bombing and subsequent

---
31. Suarez 2017, p256.
32. ibid., p7.
33. Hammer 2009, p48.

Zionist occupation of his village. They were forced north toward the refugee camps in Lebanon. Shortly after their arrival, his sister died from heat exhaustion. "My mother would sit by her grave every day, lost in grief."[34]

In 1948 alone, between 750,000 and 900,000 Palestinians were expelled from their land, and refugees were forcibly prevented from returning to their homes after the fog of war had lifted. The British rewarded Zionist terror by accelerating their withdrawal and offering more concessions to the Zionists.

At midnight on 14 May 1948, the leaders of the Zionist organisations in Palestine, headed by David Ben-Gurion, proclaimed the establishment of the state of Israel. The US recognised the provisional Zionist government as the de facto authority in Israel within minutes. It was swiftly followed by the Soviet Union, which was one of the most committed to the Zionist project. The mistaken characterisation of Stalinist USSR as socialist by the majority of the left led many to follow its lead in defending the foundation of the Israeli state.

On 15 May 1948, the new state of Israel was declared and recognised by the UN. This is why, while 15 May is Israel's national day, Palestinians mourn their loss and fight for restitution. It is called the Nakba, or the "catastrophe", by Palestinians and their supporters.

---

34. Jonathan Cook, "Nakba Survivors Share their Stories of Loss and Hope", *Dissident Voice*, 19 May 2016.
    https://dissidentvoice.org/2016/05/nakba-survivors-share-their-stories-of-loss-and-hope/.

CHAPTER THREE

Israel and Imperialism

Imperialism is an expression of the tension inherent in capitalist competition writ on an international scale. It is not simply military rivalry, nor is it merely the rule of large, powerful nation-states over smaller ones. Rather, it is the global system of competition between blocs of capital organised into nation-states. Powerful nation-states attempt to control, rule and shape the world. This can involve economic institutions like the World Bank or the International Monetary Fund, diplomatic and political institutions like the United Nations, or the naked use of violence through military conflict.

The balance of forces in this global chess game has changed throughout history. Before the end of the Second World War, the imperial order was multipolar. The main imperial battles were between the similarly sized powers of Western Europe plus the rising power of the USA. After World War Two the main imperial rivalry was between the Cold War antagonists, the USSR and the USA. Between them, the world was divided into competing blocs. When the USSR collapsed, the global imperial set-up was dominated by the United States. But global capitalism is not a static system. It is constantly changing, as old powers give way to new ones and the relative strength of rival states waxes and wanes. It is impossible

After 1948

Israel was established as a recognised state on the world stage in 1948. After the declaration of Israeli statehood, UN endorsement and the evacuation of the British, a number of the surrounding Arab states felt the need to intervene into the changing political situation. While they framed their military intervention in terms of solidarity with the Palestinians, in reality they were hoping to annex for themselves as much Palestinian land as possible. The Arab armies (of Iraq, Jordan, Syria, Lebanon and Egypt) fielded around 100,000 troops for what became known as the First Arab-Israeli war, but they were ill-equipped and badly trained. In contrast, the Zionist forces had managed to get military equipment from the Eastern bloc, as the USSR was courting Israel and hoping to bring it into the fold. Battles between these forces raged between May and November of 1948, as the boundaries of the future state were at stake. By the end of the war, the Arab armies had been pushed back: Egypt controlled the Gaza Strip while Jordan took the West Bank and East Jerusalem. A whole series of towns and cities outside the UN mandate were captured by Israel and annexed into its body politic.

Victories in the military field encouraged Israel to push on the diplomatic and economic fronts. It demanded and received from the British all the taxes that were collected during the mandate period, from both Palestinians and Zionists. This added substantially to the coffers of the new state. The USSR, Britain and the USA all sent diplomatic envoys to Tel Aviv, further cementing Israel's relationships with a number of the big imperial powers. Israel was thus an important regional player from the very start.

The subsequent history of Israel was to be shaped by three important dynamics: a deeply aggressive antagonistic relationship with the Palestinians, the imperial conflicts in the Middle East and the growing nationalist movements in the region. All three of these factors would impact on and shape one another.

By the end of the Nakba and the Arab-Israeli war, Israeli aggression had created over a million Palestinian refugees. Almost all of them lived in camps near the borders of Palestine. The camps were controlled by the United Nations Relief and Works Agency (UNRWA) and were, according to Ilan Pappé, "the brainchild of American entrepreneurs who were not interested directly in the political dimensions of the refugee problem, but believed they could link the refugees' settlement in Arab countries with a kind of Marshall Plan for the Middle East. As in Europe, the idea was to promote better standards of living as the best means for containing Soviet expansion."[1] This "better standard of living" never eventuated, as the camps – initially canvas tents, then mudbrick houses – became squalid and poverty-stricken enclaves. The host states, mainly Lebanon, Syria and Jordan, were far from hospitable. In Lebanon Palestinians were excluded from over 40 occupational categories and discriminated against in housing and employment. In Jordan the monarchy attempted to assimilate Palestinians while maintaining a vice-like grip on their political organisations. These regimes were, rightly as it would turn out, concerned about the potentially radicalising impact of the Palestinian population. The mere existence of these refugees would have a major impact on the politics of the region. They added a volatile, socially unstable element.

The project of ethnically cleansing the Palestinians from Israel continued apace after 1948. In 1950 the Knesset passed legislation allowing the government to confiscate Palestinian land, villages and property and to use it for "Jewish public purposes".[2] Alongside this legal injunction there were grassroots movements, like the kibbutzim, that occupied the land. Forty Palestinian villages were

---

1. Pappé 2008, p143.
2. ibid., p147.

depopulated between 1949 and 1952. The populations were moved to other villages, planted in other countries or dispersed internally. This process of land theft and population movement was to be an ongoing element of Israel's policy.

There were broader factors at play too. The politics of the Cold War were acted out on the battleground of the Middle East, with Israel as a key player. All the big powers were competing for allies in the region to guarantee their trade routes, their oil supplies and their economic interests. Reports at the time stressed the importance to the West of Middle East oil resources, which represented an estimated 75 percent of proven reserves outside the Russian bloc. What's more, if the Cold War were to turn hot, the Middle East would be important as a nexus between Europe, Africa and Asia. From a Western perspective, it was a suitable area from which to mount air attacks against Russia and from which to protect the right flank of NATO. It stood in the way of a Russian outlet to the Indian Ocean through the Persian Gulf, and Russian penetration of the African continent through the Sinai Peninsula.[3] Initially the US considered Saudi Arabia the lynchpin of the region. A State Department communiqué in 1945 described the country as "a stupendous source of strategic power, and one of the greatest material prizes in world history".[4] Nevertheless gaining Israel's loyalty would be important on both sides of the Iron Curtain.

The rising tide of nationalism

World War Two marked the beginning of the end of Western European colonial power. Across the world a number of anti-colonial movements exploded in its aftermath. In 1951 a new government in Iran led by Dr Mohammad Mossadeq nationalised British oil interests. Protests and strikes by students and workers erupted in Egypt and Lebanon. Left nationalist parties rapidly grew in influence, culminating in the 1952 revolution in Egypt. These developments

---

3. Reich 2002, p42.
4. Chomsky 1999, p17.

were of deep concern to the Western powers, which sought to shore up their interests any way they could. Israel offered its services as a gun for hire: defending the stability and security of Western interests in the region. In 1951 Gershom Shocken, the editor of Israel's leading newspaper *Haaretz*, outlined what would become Israel's *raison d'être* throughout the twentieth century:

> Strengthening Israel helps the Western powers to maintain equilibrium and stability in the Middle East. Israel is to become the watchdog. There is no fear that Israel will undertake any aggressive policy towards the Arab states when these would explicitly contradict the wishes of US and Britain. But if for any reasons the Western powers should sometimes wish to close their eyes, Israel could be relied upon to punish one or several neighbouring states whose discourtesy to the West went beyond the bounds of the permissible.[5]

For the Zionist leadership, strengthening Israel required expansion. Not content with the borders established after the defeat of the Arab armies, Israeli prime minister David Ben-Gurion was perpetually on the lookout for ways to expand Israeli territory. By the mid-1950s Israel felt confident to begin exploiting the nationalist tensions in the surrounding countries.

In Egypt, Gamal Abdel Nasser had come to power on the back of a nationalist revolt of disaffected military and popular outrage against the British. In July of 1956 his government nationalised the prized Suez Canal. Previously owned and managed by a joint British-French company, the canal was a vital route for global trade, described by one historian as the "artery for oil tankers bound for the West".[6] This flagrant disregard for their interests terrified the old European powers, who feared that it might inspire other anti-colonial movements. The French were in the middle of a brutal war against nationalist forces in Algeria and worried that Nasser's Egypt would weigh in against them. So the French, the British and Israel joined forces and launched an assault on Nasser's government. The French made a series of secret deals which consolidated Israel's

5. Rose 2004, p155.
6. ibid., p156.

militarisation and power. While ultimately the Israeli, British and French attempts to unseat Nasser were unsuccessful, the Suez crisis marked Israel out as a major military player in the region. Just a few years later a US National Security Council Memorandum would note that a "logical corollary" of opposition to radical Arab nationalism "would be to support Israel as the only strong pro-West power left in the near East".[7]

1967 and the "favoured regime"

By the beginning of the 1960s, Israel was still jostling with other pro-Western states – Turkey, the Shah's Iran and the Gulf monarchies – for the privilege of being America's key ally. In the 1967 war it proved itself up to the task of being the region's main bully by decimating the armies of Jordan, Syria and Egypt. Pappé describes it thus:

> In a classical example of a blitzkrieg, a highly motivated and professional Israeli army exploited the element of surprise and used its superior Western arms to great advantage, exposing the inferiority of the Arab countries' Eastern bloc military equipment.[8]

America's watchdog had proved itself a pit bull. By the end of six days of war, Israel had captured the West Bank, the Gaza Strip, the Golan Heights, the whole of Jerusalem and the Sinai Peninsula. This of course meant further dispossession of the Palestinians, and the events of 1967 became known as the Naksa or the "setback". In the West Bank, 55 percent of the land and 70 percent of the water were seized for the benefit of Jewish settlers, who constituted only a tiny fraction of the population. In Gaza, 2,200 settlers were given more than 40 percent of the land, while 500,000 Palestinians were confined to crowded slums and camps.[9] The occupation of the West Bank and Gaza saw an intensification of the oppression of the Palestinians, another factor that shaped Palestinian resistance over the coming decades.

7. Chomsky 1999, p21.
8. Pappé 2004, p188.
9. Gasper 2002, p27.

What's more, Israel's military victory against Nasser in Egypt assured the West that Israel could play an absolutely central role in keeping various nationalist Arab regimes under control. A US State Department document said:

> Israel has probably done more for the US in the Middle East in relation to money and effort invested than any of our so-called allies and friends elsewhere around the world since the Second World War. In the Far East we can get almost nobody to help us in Vietnam. Here the Israelis won the war, single-handedly, have taken us off the hook and have served our interests as well as theirs.[10]

Israel had proved its military prowess. While previously the US had hedged its bets, Israel now became the favoured regime: one that could both help guarantee US economic interests and encircle any pro-Soviet or nationalist governments in the region. With blood still dripping from its jaws, Israel got a big pat on the head from the US. After 1967, US funding for Israel rose by 450 percent. Between 1967 and 1972, total US aid to Israel jumped from $13.1 million per year to $600.8 million per year. The US Congress even allowed the Pentagon to hand some of its most advanced weaponry to Israel without expecting any payment.[11]

Sometimes this support is explained through reference to a powerful Jewish lobby that has convinced the US to act against its own interests. Nothing could be further from the truth. US support for Israel is based on a cynical assessment of its strategic value in a region that is home to two-thirds of the world's oil reserves. Political and economic control over the Middle East has given the US leverage over its imperial rivals. Maintaining the stability of this beneficial set-up means suppressing any threat to its interests in the region. In the twentieth century, these threats came in the guise of Arab nationalist movements, which for a time challenged the unabashed rule of Western capital. These movements were all the

---

10. Rose 2004, p157.
11. Dave Rory, "Denounced for telling the truth", *Socialist Worker (US)*, 26 January 2007. https://socialistworker.org/2007-1/616/616_11_Carter.php.

more concerning in that they were supported by sizeable sections of the Arab working class, who saw the links between their miserable social conditions and the broader systems of colonial domination. As a result, every US administration from Truman onwards has set itself against the possibility of the development of independent centres of power in the region, thwarting the democratic wishes of the people on numerous occasions. Israel made itself central to this project by playing a key role in the suppression of every development that threatened US hegemony.

Subcontracting terror

Israel's role as a subcontractor of violence and terror wasn't limited to the Middle East. The US had a variety of authoritarian, brutal regimes across the world that it supported, though it preferred to keep these relationships quiet. It would make it harder for the US to proclaim its role as pre-eminent democratic power if it was publicly propping up dictatorships. Israel would play a very important role here. It could funnel aid and weapons to said regimes while providing diplomatic cover for the US. Since 1948 every pro-US dictatorship has received some kind of support from Israel.

A few examples will suffice. After decades of universal support, during the 1980s a number of states began to turn publicly against South African apartheid. Israel bucked the trend and maintained close ties with the regime right up until its overthrow in the 1990s. Israel trained South African military and police forces, with one Israeli newspaper reporting that "[i]t is a clear and open secret known to everybody that in [South African] army camps one can find Israeli officers in not insignificant numbers who are busy teaching white soldiers to fight Black terrorists with methods imported from Israel."[12] Israel also refused to place sanctions on the apartheid regime and funnelled arms to it right to the end. This was no aberration: Israel sent secret military advisers to aid and support

---

12. Cockburn and Cockburn 1991, p300.

African dictators such as Mobutu Sese Seko in Zaire, Idi Amin in Uganda and Ian Smith in Rhodesia.[13]

Israel's role in Latin America was similarly appalling. From 1976 to 1983 a far-right junta ruled Argentina, backed by the Reagan administration. Tens of thousands of leftists and resisters were killed or disappeared. Despite the often openly anti-Semitic nature of these killings, Israel sold arms to the regime. In Nicaragua Israel funnelled weaponry to right-wing terror groups, while in Honduras and El Salvador it sold missiles, fighter jets and armoured vehicles to regimes threatened by democratic movements. In Asia, Israel backed the deadly dictatorship of Suharto in Indonesia and supported the US-backed Marcos dictatorship in the Philippines.

Israel and the Lebanese Civil War

By the early 1970s Israel had proven its value to the US. In the years 1978 through to 1982 Israel received 48 percent of all US military aid and 35 percent of US economic aid worldwide.[14] This did not mean however that Israel only acted at the behest of the US. It continued to have its own interests: the Zionist state had not forgotten its ambitions of a Greater Israel. This ambition required a simultaneous offensive against the surrounding states as well as against Palestinians and their resistance organisations. A brief discussion of the Lebanon war illuminates Israel's counter-revolutionary role in this period.

The refugees from the Nakba and the Naksa fled in significant numbers to Lebanon, and by the 1980s the Palestinian population in the south of the country had begun to develop its own networks of support and control – a "state within a state". Led and organised by the Palestine Liberation Organisation (PLO), the refugee population built up a significant power base with its international headquarters in West Beirut. It was from here that much of the post-Naksa resistance was organised. Such political organising was

---

13. Chomsky 1999, pp67-68.
14. Rose 2004, p160.

considered a serious threat to Israel, as the PLO was launching attacks on both Israeli territory and on Israeli representatives abroad. Furthermore, the Israeli state wanted to land a major blow against the Palestinians, so it mounted pressure on the United States to back it in attempting to wipe out the PLO. Ariel Sharon, special aide to the then government, had grander ambitions. He wanted to wipe out the PLO, unseat the Syrian forces in Lebanon and install a Maronite (Christian) pro-Israeli government.

These were Israel's own ambitions: unlike in the Suez war, it was not acting at the behest of another power. It did, however, want the aid of the US in this project. Sharon visited the US in the months leading up to the Israeli invasion and made Israel's desires very clear. The US figured that backing Israel in this would ensure ongoing support for America's own projects in the region. In the first three months of 1982, military supplies from the US to Israel surged.

Israel invaded Lebanon and the results were catastrophic. West Beirut was destroyed in carpet-bombing raids and 19,000 Lebanese and Palestinians were killed. Over 30,000 civilians were wounded in just six weeks. The world reeled in horror after reports were released of the massacres of hundreds of refugees at the Sabra and Shatila camps in September 1982. Journalist Robert Fisk was one of the first reporters on the scene:

> Down a laneway to our right, no more than 50 yards from the entrance, there lay a pile of corpses. There were more than a dozen of them, young men whose arms and legs had been wrapped around each other in the agony of death. All had been shot at point-blank range through the cheek, the bullet tearing away a line of flesh up to the ear and entering the brain. Some had vivid crimson or black scars down the left side of their throats. One had been castrated, his trousers torn open and a settlement of flies throbbing over his torn intestines.[15]

While the Israeli military didn't commit these massacres themselves, they were more than complicit. Israeli military personnel stood around the camps watching on as the Phalangists, a fascistic

---
15. Fisk 1992, p361.

paramilitary outfit, completed their bloody work, firing flares into the air to facilitate the killings well into the night. The US, despite mealy-mouthed criticisms after the fact, was also complicit; it reneged on an agreement to facilitate the safe evacuation of Palestinians from the camps. Furthermore, in a pattern that was to become painfully familiar, the US failed to translate its rhetorical objections to Israeli war crimes into anything more substantial.

The invasion of Lebanon demonstrates that Israel is not merely a puppet of its imperial backers. As a state, it has its own agenda: the seizure of more and more land. The destruction of Palestinian resistance and any regional hostility is a necessary pre-condition for the achievement of this goal. American backing is necessary and welcome but is not always the driving force. The US has *its* own agenda. It wants to maintain its economic and military power and stability for American capital. In most instances US and Israeli interests align, but on occasion there are divergences. These tensions are not based on any moral quandaries that the US might have with Israel's behaviour, or vice versa. Instead they are driven by a desire to allow the fullest and freest flourishing of US interests. Sometimes Israel's hostilities and brutalities (towards the Palestinians in particular) can be too provocative, too destabilising. So for instance the US refused to call on Israel to participate actively in the 1991 Gulf War. It feared that if Israel intervened, the US's carefully constructed coalition, which included various Arab regimes, would collapse. It is important to understand that these breaches of unanimity are no more than a lovers' quarrel. They represent tensions in the manner of regional domination rather than any substantive cleavage over who should actually be the dominant force.

The US wants to maintain relationships with other Arab regimes. Oftentimes historically, hostilities by Israel toward the Palestinian struggles have prompted disruptions in other Middle Eastern countries. To this end, the US has positioned itself as a champion of negotiations and peaceful dialogue between the Palestinians and Israel. The lie that the US is interested in peace is one of the most egregious in twentieth-century history and will be discussed in more detail in chapter 4. Suffice it to say here, the years of "peace negotiations" amounted to nothing more than a palatable ideological cover for the ongoing expansion of Israeli control over Palestinian territory, an entrenching of US power in the region and the enrichment of a minority of Palestinians.

The War on Terror

While the 1990s were good years for the US, Israel and a burgeoning Palestinian bourgeoisie, the situation for ordinary Palestinians was becoming unbearable. War criminal Ariel Sharon was elected prime minister of Israel in March 2001, reflecting the strengthening of right-wing forces in Israeli politics. The Palestinian offensives, launched by new, more Islamist-oriented forces, came a year before the attacks on the New York twin towers on 9/11, after which the new global "War on Terror" was declared. US military offensives were launched in Afghanistan in 2001 and more were promised. US president George W. Bush traced an "axis of evil" across the globe, from Iraq to Syria to North Korea. This axis was to be demolished militarily, one country after the other. Neo-conservatives in the US administration were explicit in their intention to reassert what they saw as waning US power across the world.

The War on Terror gave an ideological licence to the Israeli state to go on the offensive against the Palestinian territories. Just days after September 11 the Israelis launched incursions into Jenin in the West Bank and into Gaza. Twenty-one Palestinians were killed in days, and whole suburbs were flattened. Israel justified this response by positioning itself as the victim of Islamic terror. This charge had new force in the context of a West that had largely accepted the premise of the war: that Islamic fundamentalism led to terrorism and was the dominant problem in the world. Five weeks after September 11, the Israeli state occupied Palestinian towns and villages. It also strengthened and lengthened the sieges and curfews imposed over all the Occupied Territories. Ariel Sharon declared that the Palestinian Authority was "an entity which supports terror", and George W. Bush endorsed this statement by saying that "Israel had the right to defend itself". In doing so, Bush gave the green light to Israel to launch a major offensive. A new round of assassinations of Palestinian leaders occurred. In April of 2002, as part of an attempt to break Palestinian resistance and further control Palestinian territory, Sharon ordered an attack on the Jenin refugee camp in the West Bank. What followed was yet another horrific example of the cold and calculating nature of Israeli terror. The Israeli army sealed off the entire area around Jenin and refused to allow anyone in or out as helicopter gunships pulverised the town. Journalists and government officials were allowed in after the massacre occurred. Even hardened war reporters were shocked. Janine di Giovani from the *Times* wrote:

> The refugees I had interviewed in recent days were not lying. If anything they underestimated the carnage. Rarely – in more than a decade of war reporting from Bosnia, Chechnya, Sierra Leone, Kosovo – have I seen such deliberate destruction, such disrespect for human life. I have seen demolished houses before. I have seen wells stuffed with bodies. I have seen civilians terrorised and living under siege. But what remains of Jenin camp is a wasteland of death.[16]

In 2003 the US invaded Iraq and opened a new and devastating chapter in Middle Eastern politics, the after-effects of which are still being felt. Israel backed the US war down the line. Prominent Israeli politicians were falling over themselves to mount a case for taking out Hussein's regime. Benjamin Netanyahu declared, "Today nothing less than dismantling his regime will do" and "I believe I speak for the overwhelming majority of Israelis in supporting a pre-emptive strike against Saddam's regime".[17] Here US and Israeli interests coincided. The US had a grand plan to re-assert American military power across the world, and Israel had a desire to destroy

---

16. Cited in "Palestine: The evidence that no-one can ignore", *Socialist Worker* (UK), 20 April 2002.
   https://socialistworker.co.uk/art/6958/Palestine%3A+the+evidence+nobody+can+ignore.
17. Benjamin Netanyahu, "The case for toppling Saddam", *Wall Street Journal*, 20 September 2002.

regimes in the region that were hostile to US and therefore Israeli interests. Meanwhile the Israeli forces were working to assert themselves regionally against other both pro- and anti-Western powers. Israel offered the US "evidence" of Iraqi weapons of mass destruction and played up the international threat. The irony of the only Middle Eastern power with nuclear weapons concerning itself with other countries' putative military threat was palpable.

Despite declaring "mission accomplished" on 1 May 2003, George W. Bush was discovering that pacifying an entire country was more difficult than anticipated. By 2005, the Western imperial forces found themselves in a protracted, bloody conflict. Other regional powers were starting to grow in strength and, while the US was floundering, they were using the opportunity to grow their own power and prestige. The US was the big dog, but the other, smaller dogs were growing stronger and starting to strain at the leash. Israel was deeply concerned by the rise of other regional powers, particularly Iran, and was seeking ways to challenge this power and reassert its own military strength. It was in this context that Israel launched an attack on Lebanon in the summer of 2006.

The 2006 Lebanon War

Israel had long had a desire to gain more territory by occupying surrounding countries and annexing such land into Greater Israel. After the 1982 invasion, Israel occupied large parts of Lebanon but found by the mid-1980s that a full-scale, ongoing occupation of the country required a huge outlay of resources. It withdrew to the South. Here, in the area closest to Israel and Palestine, the majority of the population is Shia. While the Israelis had a long-term strategy of attempting to foment divisions between the Shia and the Palestinians, dividing and ruling both, by the late 1990s a resentful, impoverished and oppressed Shia population had built up a resistance force in the form of Hezbollah. In 2000 Hezbollah managed to push Israel out of the South. In the rest of the country

ISRAEL AND IMPERIALISM

the broader imperial battles were played out. After the civil war in Lebanon ended in 1989, the Syrians stayed, dominating politically and occupying militarily. The tensions and interplays between the US, Israel, Syria, Iran and the other regional powers are too complex to enter into here; suffice it to say by 2003 both Israel and the US were keen to push Syria out of Lebanon and defang Hezbollah. The US and Israel pushed the UN to adopt a resolution to this effect in September 2004. In March 2005 Syria withdrew 14,000 troops but Hezbollah was still armed, active and popular. It ran South Lebanon, much like the PLO had earlier, as a state within a state. And so, under the pretext of recapturing two kidnapped Israeli soldiers, Israel began bombardments of Lebanon in July 2006. This was followed by a ground invasion of the South a few days later. The US gave a green light to any barbarity Israel chose to employ. At a press conference on July 21 2006, Secretary of State Condoleezza Rice stated:

> What we're seeing here…is the growing – the "birth pangs" – of a "New Middle East" and whatever we do we have to be certain that we're pushing forward to the New Middle East [and] not going back to the old one.[18]

But despite its dramatically superior military power, Israel failed to defeat Hezbollah. Lebanese Marxist historian Gilbert Achcar said, after the conclusion of the war:

> Hizbollah could not inflict a major military defeat on Israel, a possibility that was always excluded by the utterly disproportionate balance of forces in the same way that it was impossible for the Vietnamese resistance to inflict a major military defeat on the US; but neither could Israel inflict any defeat on Hizbollah. In this sense, Hizbollah is undoubtedly the real political victor and Israel the real loser in the 33-day war.[19]

This was a major political defeat for Israel. For the first time in decades it, in league with its patrons at the White House, was unable to dominate and shape the contours of the Arab world to its will. More broadly, Hezbollah's victory laid the basis for a significant

---
18. Cited in Kaplan 2006.
19. Cited in Harman 2006.

growth in its prestige across the Middle East. This gave its allies, like Hamas, some reflected glory.

Gaza 2009–10

By the late 2000s Israel was becoming increasingly concerned with the consolidation of Hamas' prestige in the Gaza strip. After managing to subdue and co-opt much of the Palestinian leadership in the West Bank, this new force did not seem quite as pliant. Furthermore, Hamas was connected to Iran, a fact that worried Israel greatly. In January 2006 Hamas won the elections in Gaza. This victory had a disquieting effect on both the US and Israel. One US Department of Defense operative revealed the nature of the response: "Everyone blamed everyone else. We sat there in the Pentagon [after the election] and said, 'Who the fuck recommended this [Palestinian elections]?'"[20] Both Washington and Jerusalem were worried that the "Hamas effect" would hit Amman and Cairo, two of the most vital centres of pro-Western power in the region. In 2007 Israel imposed an extremely punitive blockade on Gaza; this monstrous policy was followed up in 2009 with its bombardment of the Strip.

While Hamas was not destroyed by this bombardment, its operations were severely curtailed. Israel was not content to rest however, and has continued the siege of Gaza, conducted regular bombing raids, and launched another major offensive in 2014.

Arab revolution and counter-revolution

In the *Communist Manifesto* Karl Marx famously said "all that is solid melts into air". In January 2011 the apparently solid, ossified, authoritarian regimes across the Arab world seemed to melt before the heat of the popular uprisings. Millions of ordinary people swept into the streets and squares of Tunisia and the old regime crumbled. In Egypt, the occupation of Tahrir Square, the strike wave that engulfed key industries and the ransacking and destruction of sites of the regime's power shook the foundations of the

---

20. Haddad 2009.

30-year-old dictatorship of Hosni Mubarak. The joy and beauty of these democratic uprisings inspired similar revolts, from Bahrain to Libya to Syria. Ruling classes were terrified and scrambled to find a way of reasserting their control. The Israeli ruling class was particularly concerned. Israeli defence minister Ehud Barak said that the region had been hit by "a historic earthquake" and that Israel faced a political "tsunami".[21] They had reason to be fearful. Israeli regional strength was bolstered and maintained not only by its own military power and its relationship with the US, but also by its relationships with other sympathetic regimes. Since the détente in the 1970s, Israel and Egypt had developed close ties. Indeed, one Israeli journalist, Aluf Benn, wrote: "Of all the world's statesmen the one closest to [Israeli] Prime Minister Benjamin Netanyahu is Egyptian President Hosni Mubarak".[22]

Historically the fates of resistance movements across the Middle East have been intimately entwined with the fate of the Palestinian movement. A popular uprising across the Arab world could inspire a resumption of the Palestinian resistance known as the Intifada. The regional ruling classes and interested imperial parties elsewhere in the world (the US and Russia) began to move against the uprisings. A variety of counter-revolutionary tactics were used – from fomenting sectarian division, to buying the allegiance of previously oppositional forces, to simply, as in the Syrian example, drowning the revolutionary movement in blood. While the process is still unfolding, the Arab Spring and the subsequent counter-revolution have revealed some of the changing imperial dynamics that are at play. These new situations invariably impact Israel.

US socialist Ashley Smith summarises the new imperial reality when he says:

> [As] a result of defeats in Iraq and Afghanistan and the Great Recession, Washington has suffered relative geopolitical and economic decline, allowing various states to challenge American dictates throughout the world system. As a result, Washington's unipolar order has given way to

21. Marfleet 2015.
22. ibid.

a new asymmetric multipolar world order. Of course, the United States remains the hegemonic state, but it now faces a new international rival in China, as well as a revived Russia intent on reclaiming its lost power, and various regional rivals like Iran.[23]

In the Middle East, the relative decline of US power has opened up the space for smaller sub-imperial powers to assert themselves. We thus see growing power and ambition from Iran, Saudi Arabia, Turkey, and of course Israel. There has been increased jockeying between these powers, either in proxy conflicts, like those in Syria, or in more obvious tensions, like those between Israel and Iran. The US on its own does not have – nor did it ever completely have – the capacity to absolutely dictate the terms on which the battles are being fought. What this means for Israel remains to be seen, but at the very least, we can be sure that Israel's ambitions for a Greater Israel remain. The Palestinians, as always, will be the first victims of these imperial goals.

---

23. Smith 2018.

CHAPTER FOUR

Oslo and Beyond: the Lie of Peace

One of the most used and abused terms in Middle Eastern politics is "peace". As in George Orwell's dystopian novel 1984, political words often mean their opposite in imperial power play: peace is war, war is peace. Thus the United States and Israel, two of the most belligerent and violent nations on the planet, are somehow transformed into brokers of peace. Unfortunately, sections of the Palestinian movement have become complicit in the peddling of this lie. This chapter will look at the origins of the idea of a US orchestrated peace process, how it has manifested itself over time and how and why sections of the Palestinian leadership have signed what is effectively their own death warrant.

The origins of US "peace"

During the Cold War, the US developed an important false ideological narrative in which it was a democratic nation wielding justice and bringing peace to the world. In the Middle East it offered itself as a supposedly honest broker between warring parties, but in reality it was no such force. All its actions were designed to undermine the power of the USSR and strengthen its own. Israel was an important lynchpin in this agenda.

By the 1970s previously "independent" nationalist regimes were beginning to orient more toward Western capital, and the US took full advantage. In 1978, the US, under Democrat Jimmy Carter, managed to broker a landmark deal between Egypt and Israel called the Camp David Accords. The result was to normalise Israel as a legitimate state among the other Arab states and also to broaden the states in the region that operated within the US sphere of influence. The Accords also formally granted Palestinians "autonomy" in the West Bank. But, just like the word "peace," in the world of US-brokered negotiations, "autonomy" for the Palestinians has never meant genuine self-control. Noam Chomsky describes the situation thus:

The status of the Palestinians has been even lower than that of other worthless people; their value is not zero, but negative in that their plight has a disruptive effect in the Arab world, thus interfering with US goals. They must therefore be marginalised somehow, perhaps under a form of "autonomy" that leaves them to manage their own affairs under Israeli supervision.[1]

The Palestinian leadership under Arafat accepted, almost without question, the crumbs of autonomy that were granted them from the Accords. The scene was set for further capitulation.

Oslo

The next round of major talks began in 1993 after the end of the Palestinian uprising known as the First Intifada. These talks were known as the Oslo Accords and signalled an important moment in the death spiral of the Fatah-led Palestine Liberation Organisation.

For decades, various Israeli leaders had developed schemes for the reorganisation of Palestinian oppression. From the Allon plan of 1967, to the Labour Party Settlement Plan of 1976, to the Sharon plan of 1992, they all involved giving the Palestinians small

---

1. Chomsky 1999, p535.

pieces of territory in which they could "autonomously" govern themselves. This so-called autonomy would be, as US journalist Danny Rubenstein described, the "autonomy of a POW camp, where the prisoners are 'autonomous' to cook their own meals without interference and to organise cultural events".[2]

The conclusion of the Cold War, the subsequent realignment of power in the region and the Camp David Accords meant that the US and Israel felt in a strong position to push home their advantage. The Palestinian leadership was weak, already deeply compromised and primed to accept whatever appalling deal was put on the table in front of them.

In exchange for Israeli withdrawal from Gaza and the bulk of the West Bank (in which an "autonomous" Palestinian Authority would be established), the Palestinian leadership was asked to accept Israel's right to exist within the borders developed in 1967. Such an agreement would mean abandoning the rights of the Palestinian refugees who were expelled in 1948, as well as those who had lost their homes and territories in 1967.

PLO leader Arafat couldn't be seen to accept such an abject capitulation too easily and so the negotiations continued for two years. The second iteration of Oslo was eventually agreed upon in 1995. It divided up the West Bank into three zones of territorial control: A, B and C. Each would have different rulers. In zone A (about three percent of the West Bank), a Palestinian National Authority (PA) would have total control, in zone C (about 75 percent of the West Bank) Israel would exercise control, while in zone B (about 23 percent of the West Bank) the PA would administer Palestinian villages under Israel's "security control".[3] Jerusalem was to be under Israeli control. Furthermore, Oslo II also pushed the Palestinians to accept all current and future Israeli settlements in zone B. In essence what the whole agreement amounted to was a subtle and slow consolidation of control over the whole of historic Palestine.

---

2. ibid., p535.
3. Beinin 1999. (Figures given are for 1995.)

The PLO became subcontractors for Israel. The policing of the Palestinian population would be outsourced in large parts of the West Bank to the Palestinian Authority. The Palestinian Preventative Security force, a body overseen by Fatah member Mohammed Dahlan, had over 20,000 people under arms. Its role was to police, corral and intimidate any political forces in the West Bank or Gaza who might oppose Fatah. For instance, in 1994 confrontations between the PA and Hamas activists ended in the murder of 14 Hamas members. Two years later the PA was responsible for rounding up hundreds of Islamist activists under suspicion of bombings in Israel. The PA was clearly doing the work of the Israeli state. Palestinian scholar Edward Said wrote of the abject capitulation that was Oslo:

> Now that some of the euphoria has lifted, it is possible to re-examine the Israeli-PLO agreement with the required common sense. What emerges from such scrutiny is a deal that is more flawed...than many had first supposed. The fashion-show vulgarities of the White House ceremony, the degrading spectacle of Yasser Arafat thanking everyone for the suspension of most of his people's rights, and the fatuous solemnity of Bill Clinton's performance, like a twentieth-century Roman emperor shepherding two vassal kings through rituals of reconciliation and obeisance: all these only temporarily obscure the truly astonishing proportions of the Palestinian capitulation. So first of all let us call the agreement by its real name: an instrument of Palestinian surrender, a Palestinian Versailles.[4]

The establishment of the Palestinian Authority saw the development of a corrupt and bureaucratised Palestinian elite – an elite that was tied to Fatah and increasingly to Israel. The growth of this new capitalist class was dependent on monopolising government contracts. Adam Hanieh described this process well in 2003:

> [The capitalist class derives] its wealth from a privileged relationship with the PA, which assisted its growth by granting monopolies for goods like cement, petroleum, flour, steel and cigarettes; issuing exclusive import permits and customs exemptions; giving sole rights to distribute goods in the West Bank and Gaza Strip; and distributing government-owned land below its value.

---

4. Said 2003.

> In addition to these state-assisted forms of accumulation, much of the investment that came into the West Bank was from foreign donors. Through the Oslo years – infrastructure construction, new building projects, agricultural and tourist developments – were also typically connected to this new capitalist class in some way.[5]

Such a situation led to huge pools of wealth concentrated in the hands of a minority. For instance, Mohammad Dahlan, the head of the security force, built a palace in Gaza so ornate that it sunk into the sand from the weight of its marble and gold. Meanwhile the class divide was widening. The UN estimated that throughout this period 80 percent of Gazans lived below the poverty line.

So by the end of the 1990s, a Palestinian elite was basking in riches derived from dirty dealing with the US and Israel. Meanwhile the Palestinian movement was being disarmed and disoriented. The wind was knocked out of any serious mass Palestinian resistance movement and it was incapable of resisting new offences against them. The after-effects were disastrous. The Oslo years saw a massive expansion of Israeli settlements. The number of Jewish settlers living in the Occupied Territories grew exponentially from 1993. Settlement building was accompanied by the building of a labyrinthine number of "bypass roads" which fragmented the territory. These roads link the "territories under Israeli control so that settlers can travel freely without having to see the Arab villages scattered in the hills, or the municipal areas run by the PA".[6]

Academic Naseer Aruri put it clearly when he wrote:

> Historically, colonial settler movements relied mostly on military conquests, population expulsion, land alienation, and even genocide to accomplish their goals of ethnic cleansing. While Israel has been no exception, having tried most of these reprehensible methods, Oslo is the first diplomatic arrangement that has permitted it to make tangible colonial achievements with minimum reliance on its armed forces.[7]

Such a situation could only occur because of the compliance of

---

5. Hanieh 2013.
6. Chomsky 1999, p545.
7. Aruri 2002, p89.

Fatah, which was now a consolidating ruling class in the West Bank, just as corrupt and tied to global capital as any bourgeoisie.

The other outcome of the Oslo accords was the rapid development of the Israeli economy. The Oslo accords allowed a normalisation between Israel and other Arab countries and also opened the door for increased levels of European investment. The *Financial Times* observed that "Israel will look back on 1995 as the year when international finance and business discovered its thriving economy".[8]

These "facts on the ground" led to increasing disillusionment amongst Palestinians with Fatah and the existing political formations. This disillusionment exploded into active resistance in the Second Intifada in 2000 but unfortunately the sham of "peace talks" was not consigned to history.

2003: The "Road Map to Peace"

While the US was launching its offensive in Iraq, it was simultaneously sponsoring a new "peace" initiative between the Israelis and Palestinians. This "Road Map to Peace" as it became known was the new cover that the US developed in order to try and quieten down the Palestinian "problem". They had a lot on their hands in Iraq and didn't want another front to open up in Palestine. Furthermore, while there was increasing disquiet internationally about the war in Iraq, the US wanted a gesture that would maintain the illusion that they were democratic peace-brokers, interested in Arab rights. While initially hostile to the plan, Ariel Sharon eventually came on board. On paper the Road Map seemed to make concessions to the Palestinians but in reality the plan was about bolstering Israeli strength. The settlement-building increased even more rapidly during the Road Map discussions. Furthermore, the talks allowed Sharon and Bush to sideline Yasser Arafat who, for all his betrayals, still had an independent Palestinian base. Mahmoud Abbas (also known as Abu Mazen) was Sharon and Bush's preferred candidate. Their determination to make Abbas a central player illustrated the

---

8. Cited in Chomsky 1999, p552.

US and Israel's confidence in their ability to mould the Palestinian leadership to their will. Abbas illustrated his complicity in speech after speech during this time, especially when he described armed resistance to Israel as "terrorism".

> Let me be very clear: There will be no military solution for this conflict, so we repeat our renunciation and the renunciation of terrorism against the Israelis wherever they might be... We will exert all of our efforts using all our resources to end the militarisation of the *intifada* and we will succeed... Our goal is clear and we will implement it firmly and without compromise: a complete end to violence and terrorism. And we will be full partners in the international war against terrorism. And we will call upon our partners in this war to prevent financial and military assistance to those who oppose this position.[9]

Such gross servility to the US and Israel could not be stomached, even by other obviously compromised sections of the Palestinian movement, and attacks on Israel increased. There was a growing distance between the leadership of the Palestinian Authority in the West Bank and the expanding forces of Hamas in Gaza. Increasingly it became clear that the road on the "map to peace" was a dead end.

Forces in Israeli politics that had previously argued against the granting of a Palestinian state started to look to the possibility of continuing to build up Israeli dominance in the West Bank while withdrawing settlements from Gaza. This project became known as the "disengagement plan", although Sharon had apparently called his plan the "separation plan" before realising that "separation sounded bad, particularly in English, because it evoked apartheid".[10] On the surface this almost looked like a step toward granting some Palestinian control over Palestinian territory. Sharon's ultimate goal was to withdraw settlements from Gaza, thereby removing any obligations or expectations that Israel would provide any services or rights to the population living in the territory. In 2005 Israel withdrew 7,000 Jewish settlers and 3,000 accompanying soldiers. After the territory became a more distinct and purely Palestinian

---
9. Marsden 2003.
10. Poole 2006, p87.

entity Sharon could proceed to isolate and eventually pulverise the Gazan population. The next few years would demonstrate just how successful this plan was to be for the Israeli state.

The lessons for the Palestinian movement should be clear. The talk of peace was, and remains, a lie. Oppressive imperialist states never act with generosity or kindness. They are not interested in a world without war and violence. The world capitalist system has gears that are greased with the blood and tears of populations like the Palestinians. Because the rich and powerful, the heads of states, are a minority, they develop weasel words, crafty ideological coverings, in order to convince oppressed populations that they are acting in our interests. Hence the use of rhetoric like "peace talks" or "humanitarian interventions". In this case the evidence is in. The years of peace negotiations sent the Palestinian cause backwards. Current and future Palestinian movements will not achieve liberation if they look to their oppressors to grant it to them. Palestinian liberation will only be won through independent revolutionary struggle.

CHAPTER FIVE
Australia and Israel

The dominant explanation for the pro-Israel consensus in Australian politics given by Australian Zionists and the political establishment is that Australia and Israel have a deep cultural affinity, based on shared experiences, values and beliefs. An Australian government pictorial history produced to celebrate the sixtieth anniversary of the establishment of Israel draws on the nationalist myths of both countries:

> Both peoples pursued their national goals with an irrepressible confidence, resourcefulness, optimism and a knack for improvisation. The immigrant experience, developing land in a harsh environment and a pioneering spirit of adventure have both featured prominently in the history of both nations. More profoundly the early Zionist pioneers and the Australian diggers of both world wars shared an ethos of social egalitarianism and a healthy irreverence for authority.[1]

In a less romantic fashion historian Colin Rubenstein makes the same point:

> Geopolitically, there is little reason to expect Australia and Israel to have a closer relationship than any other two states of a similar size

---
1. Piggot 2008.

and distance from one another. But there is something in our cultures, national outlooks and personalities drawing us together.[2]

The Israeli embassy traces this symbiosis back to the Australian military's role in Palestine in World War One:

> Many Israelis still remember the pictures of those brave men – particularly the legendary Light Horse Brigade – which fought in the crucial battles for Gaza and Beer Sheva. Memorials in Jerusalem and military cemeteries are reminders of our mutual desire for shared democratic values, liberalism, freedom and human rights.[3]

Other accounts cite the sympathy of Australian politicians towards Jewish victims of the Holocaust; the Australian ruling class was supposedly so moved by the plight of European Jewry that they made a particular effort to push the formalisation of Israel through the UN. Capitalist geopolitics, political expediency and imperialist manoeuvres are not mentioned in many of these accounts. Australian politicians are presented as paragons of conscience and generosity. Such narratives are facile at best and at worst smokescreens obscuring pragmatic colonial and imperial projects.

Some critics of the Australia-Israel relationship argue that there is a strong Israel lobby that corrals, bribes and intimidates foreign policy makers into a support for Israel they would otherwise be reluctant to give. Others argue that the genesis of Australia's support for Israel lies in the ANZUS treaty. They suggest that Australia backs Israel only because the US does. Both imply that were it not for some extraneous force, Australia would not be as committed to Israel. The well-known Jewish writer Antony Loewenstein argues: "On current evidence, the Australian government is (close to being) utterly captured by the Zionist lobby, the US alliance and blindness towards racial apartheid in the occupied territories".[4] This chapter argues against all of these claims.

---

2. Rubenstein 2008.
3. Embassy of Israel in Australia website [n.d.].
4. Loewenstein 2011. See also Burns 2010.

Colonial settler states

Both Israel and Australia began their modern lives as colonial settler states operating in regions of the world important to the most powerful capitalist countries. Both have become middle-level capitalist powers with regional aspirations to greater dominance. Both are reliant on their relationships with the biggest imperial powers of the day, first Britain and then the US. Both have been important to these powers' presence in the respective regions. The relationships have not been one-way streets, however. Both Australia and Israel have initiated mutually beneficial bargains. They have become, in the words of former Prime Minister John Howard, "deputy sheriffs" in their regions and have acquired the attendant military, economic and political power.

Countries that began as colonial settler states can play a particularly useful role for the imperialist powers. The settler populations strongly identify with the colonial power. Mainstream Australian identity is strongly Anglophile. English is indisputably the dominant language, and dominant ideological institutions encourage cultural identification with the English-speaking world. In the early history of Australia, this was with Britain; now it is with the US.

Similarly, the population of Israel sees itself as part of Western "civilisation". Culturally, most Israeli Jews identify with the West. The political, social and cultural isolation of Israel leads to a strong identification with the Zionist state. This in turn leads to a generalised support for Israel's policies towards the Palestinians. Poll after poll shows that a majority of Israelis support even the most repressive policies towards the Palestinians. These features, as explored in prior chapters, have made Israel a valuable asset for the major imperial powers.

There are many similarities between these states, but they are not the ones that the myth-makers in Australia or Israel like to highlight.

Australia, Israel and imperialism

Prior to the Second World War, Australia was firmly part of the British imperial camp, but the Australian ruling class was always straining to assert itself as a power in the region. By the time of the Second World War Australia was clearer about its own interests and pursued them with great fervour.

Australia served as part of the Allied war effort in the Middle East. This region was particularly important for Australia in terms of its strategic value – its air communications, the Suez Canal, the railway and oil pipeline from Baghdad to Haifa – and economically – the exploitation of salts from the Dead Sea. While at times the Australian government was critical of British backing for Israel, it was always on the basis of concern for Western interests. It backed almost every twist and turn of British policy, occasionally advising caution not to let support for Zionism disrupt relations with the Arab regimes. Australia was heavily invested in a stable situation in the Middle East. Historian Chanan Reich says: "The policies of Lyons and Menzies towards the Jewish-Arab conflict over Palestine were the product of a unique Australian interpretation of the interests of the British Empire in the Middle East."[5]

Zionists in Australia took a different line but continued to frame their stance in terms of what would be advantageous to Britain's and Australia's imperial interests. The president of the Victorian Jewish Advisory Board appealed to Lyons in March 1939: "Palestine is the backbone of the link between Britain and Australia and the destruction of a pro-British institution in Palestine, which the Jewish National Homeland would be, would jeopardise the communications between Australia and the Home Country".[6]

The Australian political establishment, including many Jews, saw Australian and British interests as fundamentally intertwined. Discussions in the chambers of power were never framed in moral terms; realpolitik reigned supreme. Australian

---

5. Reich 2002, p38.
6. ibid, p12.

conservatives aspired to be more British than the British. They had a long history of agitating for British interests abroad – even if this occasionally meant disagreeing with the British government. There was some conservative reluctance over Israel. The early association of Israel with Eastern European communists, the sympathy for Israel in the international labour movement and their own anti-Semitic attitudes made them suspicious of the state.[7]

The ALP, on the other hand, was much keener on a Zionist state in historic Palestine. In this, it was in accord with British Labour, which had endorsed Zionism even before the Balfour Declaration. In December 1943 the ALP national conference expressed its support for the "continued growth of the Jewish national home in Palestine by immigration and settlement".[8] One of the key figures pursuing this agenda was E.V. (Doc) Evatt, ALP leader-to-be, who was close to Zionist representatives and also wanted Australia to establish more of a presence on the world stage. He saw the international debates around Israel as a mechanism to do this. He argued that the Labor government of the day should take a more unambiguous position in favour of the partition of Palestine, the establishment of a Jewish state and the acceptance of larger numbers of Jewish settlers to Palestine. There was some reluctance in the party to go this far, but the tide was flowing in this direction.

Australia: "Godparent of the Israeli state"

World War Two left Britain militarily and economically weakened. It was proving impossible to maintain direct control over the colonies, and Britain was reconsidering the benefits of a direct mandate in Palestine. In Palestine the Zionist movement was determined to force the best possible post-colonial situation for itself. The Haganah and the Irgun launched armed offensives against British targets and terrorised Palestinians. Their violence had the intended

---

7. Labour Zionism was the left-wing current inside the Zionist movement. It encouraged Jewish workers to emigrate to Palestine to help establish a state sympathetic to workers.
8. Reich 2002, p12.

effect. The British sped up their withdrawal and offered more concessions to the Zionists.

In Australia these changes in British policy were not reflected in the position of the Liberal and Country parties. The conservatives were absolutely committed to Britain staying in Palestine; they favoured direct colonial rule. Labor shifted to a more clearly pro-Israel policy. Evatt, emboldened by a changing context, felt able to make more strident statements in support of the Zionist project. A report on a meeting he had with various Zionist representatives recorded him as launching a scathing attack on the "British policy of kowtowing to the Arabs". He said it was "disgusting in view of the Arabs' war record, when they had hung around the flanks waiting to stab us in the back if things went wrong". According to the report, Evatt also seemed somewhat forgiving in his attitude to Zionist terrorism in Palestine, arguing that it had made the world aware of the Jewish struggle.[9] He pushed for Australia to back Israel's bid for statehood, and this position won the day. He subsequently played a key role at the UN in pushing through the partition of Palestine, an act for which he is still feted by the international Zionist movement:

> Evatt's largest impact...was on the partition of Palestine, where the voting was close enough to make his enthusiastic manipulation of the rules of procedure in the Israeli cause (as chairman of the vital committee) a final feather that turned the scale. For good or ill, he may therefore be put down as one of the godfathers of the present Israeli state.[10]

At midnight on 14 May 1948, the leaders of the Zionist organisations in Palestine, headed by David Ben-Gurion, proclaimed the establishment of the state of Israel. The US recognised the provisional Zionist government as the de facto authority in Israel within minutes. It was swiftly followed by the Soviet Union. Despite its prominent role in the diplomatic manoeuvring, the Australian government took more than eight months to recognise Israel officially. On 29 January 1949, Chifley announced that the government had decided

---
9. ibid, p21.
10. Bell 1993, p54.

to give full recognition, and that it regarded the new nation as "a force of special value in the world community".[11] This declaration came a day before the British government's, but was organised in concert with it. Despite a turn towards the US, Australia had not fully broken with Britain.

The end of the Second World War saw a change in power relationships between the major imperial powers. The old European powers were overtaken by the US and the USSR who were now engaged in a major battle. The Cold War dynamic affected the entire world but had particular dynamics in different places. The expansion of Communist China was of particular regional concern to Australia. Over this period the Australian ruling class saw its interests as better guaranteed by an alliance with the US. This was formalised in 1951 with the signing of the ANZUS treaty. This treaty was not a formalisation of subservience to the US but rather a guarantee of mutual interests. Australian dominance of the Asia-Pacific region was to be maintained in return for Australian support for US expansionism elsewhere. This treaty has influenced Australian governments' attitude to the Middle East ever since.

While the US had previously hedged its bets, by 1967 it saw Israel as the favoured regime: one that could both help guarantee US economic interests and outgun any pro-Soviet governments in the region. Australia could see which way the wind was blowing. At the outbreak of the 1967 war, Prime Minister Harold Holt met with US president Lyndon Johnson in Washington and assured him that Australia would assign two of its fastest cruisers to a joint task force if it proved necessary to open the Gulf of Aqaba by force. In doing this, Australia demonstrated its allegiances. Nevertheless, Australian politicians remained concerned to keep the Arab states onside. This was a false neutrality and much more about public relations than actual support for any Arab or Muslim country.

---

11. Harris 2012.

An increasingly "special relationship"

In March 1966, the Minister of External Affairs, Paul Hasluck, was the first Australian cabinet minister to visit Israel. The Israeli daily with the largest circulation, *Ma'ariv*, "extended a warm welcome to Hasluck and praised his public support of Israel and the Zionist Federation of Australia".[12] This was followed by a flurry of joint visits and activities between the two countries, including a visit to Israel by the chairperson of the parliamentary Foreign Relations Committee, W.J. Aston, who made a pre-emptive strike in support of Israel's expansionist agenda: "I believe that, although the presence of unfriendly nations surrounding Israel has had some adverse effect, it has also spurred the people of Israel, through sheer necessity, to greater efforts".[13] Not to be outdone, the ALP opposition condemned the government for failing to act to protect the right of Israel to use the Suez Canal, or "to extend the service of the Australian airline Qantas to Israel", so "allow[ing] itself to surrender to oppression".[14]

In this period the Israeli ambassador to Australia, David Tesher, noted that in the four years of his ambassadorship, many "Australian officials, politicians, journalists and businessmen had visited Israel, including the Minister of External Affairs, the President of the Senate, the Speaker of the House of Representatives, the former and present leaders of the Opposition, the Attorney-General, the Premier of Victoria and 45 parliamentarians".[15] This practice continues today. The conservative Gorton (1968–1971) and McMahon (1971–1972) governments maintained the pro-Israel order. As *Australian Jewish News* editor Sam Lipski put it: "[W]hile John Gorton was Prime Minister, there was no question that Australia was seen to be anything but pro-Israel".[16]

The governments of the late 1960s and early 1970s have been

---
12. Reich 2002, p121.
13. ibid.
14. ibid., pp121–122.
15. Rubenstein 1987, p22.
16. ibid.

described by historians as very friendly to Israel. In the UN, Australia almost never voted in favour of resolutions severely critical of Israel, a policy that continues today. After a slight distancing from Israel under Whitlam, governments since Fraser have been unambiguously pro-Israel, despite the regular atrocities committed directly by Israel or with its complicity. Israel's war on Lebanon in 1982 is a case in point. Australia's initial response to the conflict was to excuse Israel. Malcolm Fraser argued that the offensive against Lebanon was not about crushing the Palestinian liberation movement but rather about the right of Israel to "secure and recognised boundaries".[17] Offence becomes defence and war becomes peace. A few months later, after images of Israel's strafing of Beirut emerged, Fraser argued that while the violence was to be deplored, "we need to understand that Israel suffered provocation".[18] After the massacre in the Sabra and Shatila camps, Fraser made a mealy-mouthed statement: "Events [have occurred] which weaken or diminish Israel's right to the support of countries such as Australia because it breaks down the moral position on which it stands".[19]

Fraser set the bar for excuse-making for Israel's brutality, and all Australian governments since have striven to reach it. A few key incidents suffice to illustrate the material and political support the Australian state has given Israel in recent years.

The 2006 Lebanon war

Conservative John Howard was prime minister during Israel's 2006 war on Lebanon. Among Australian prime ministers, Howard has been one of the most explicit in support of Israel. In 2002, he called himself an "unapologetic and longstanding friend of Israel".[20] In 2007, he spoke of the "personal commitment I have to the relationship between Australia and the state of Israel".[21] Under the

17. Malcolm Fraser, "Speech to the State Zionist Council on the Occasion of Israel's 34th Anniversary", 22 April 1982, cited in Rubenstein and Fleischer 2007.
18. Michelle Grattan and Stephen Mills, "Israelis Suffered Provocation on Lebanon: Fraser", *The Age*, 9 June 1982.
19. Ian Davis, "Fraser Warns Israel of Waning Support", *The Age*, 23 September 1982.
20. Cited in Rubenstein and Fleischer 2007.
21. John Howard, "Speech to the Australia-Israel Chamber of Commerce in Melbourne", 26

Howard government, Australia's UN voting record was the most pro-Israel in the world, excepting only the United States and three small Pacific Island countries. It thus came as no surprise that when Israel began its bombing campaign of Lebanon in 2006 – another offensive designed to push back a regional Arab nationalist enemy, Hezbollah – Howard was on board. Even the 1,137 civilian Lebanese deaths, 30 percent of whom were children, did not deter him. Despite the overwhelming superiority of its military and the savagery of its attack, Howard used the well-worn argument that Israel was the David against the menacing Goliaths of the region:

> Once you are attacked...and if that attack is in the context of a 50-year rejection of your right to exist, which is the situation in relation to Iran – and bear in mind the link between Iran and Hezbollah; bear in mind the exhortations from the Iranian President that Israel should be destroyed and wiped off the map – you can understand the tenacity with which the Israelis have responded.[22]

Gaza

The switch from a Howard Liberal government to a Rudd Labor government brought very little change. At no time was this more obvious than during the 2008–09 Gaza war. This offensive was designed to punish Gazans collectively for voting for a party the Israelis didn't approve of – Hamas. The offensive lasted for just under a month but killed around 1,400 Palestinians. Israel utilised the deadly chemical weapon white phosphorous, which it rained down on civilian areas of Gaza City, including a UN Relief Works Agency headquarters. Despite worldwide outrage about Israel's disproportionate use of force and anti-war demonstrations of thousands across Australia, the Labor government gave cover to the Israelis. Julia Gillard, acting prime minister at the time, blamed Hamas for the renewed violence: "Clearly the act of aggression was

---

April 2007; cited in Rubenstein and Fleischer 2007.
22. *7:30 Report*, ABC TV, 25 July 2006.
   Archived at https://web.archive.org/web/20160220105507/http://www.abc.net.au/7.30/content/2006/s1696790.htm.

engaged in by Hamas which commenced shelling with rockets and mortars into Israel," she said. "That is what breached the ceasefire, and Israel responded."[23] Prime Minister Kevin Rudd was no better:

> Australia recognises Israel's right to self-defence. The escalation in the conflict, following the [action by] Israeli ground forces, underlines the absolute importance of bringing about an effective diplomatic solution.[24]

Condemning Hamas' violence and supporting Israel's "right to self-defence" are merely ways of excusing the violence of the oppressor. When he was the Liberal opposition leader, Malcolm Turnbull insisted that Hamas must accept Israel's right to exist within secure borders. His spokesperson said he was saddened by casualties on both sides of the border, but "he noted that Hamas broke the ceasefire with its unprovoked rocket attacks on Israeli towns and villages".[25] Not one word was uttered denouncing Israel's barbaric actions. Nor were there threats to cut diplomatic relations or curb trade relations. What is more, the Australian government rejected the findings in the Goldstone Report. (This report resulted from a resolution by the United Nations Human Rights Council to investigate violations of human rights by Israel against the Palestinian people, particularly in the Gaza Strip.) On 5 November 2009 Australia voted against a UN General Assembly resolution that called, among other things, for the Goldstone Report to be sent to the UN Security Council.[26] An Australian representative told the UN General Assembly: "We have voted against this resolution because of a number of genuine concerns arising from the language of the text and the flawed nature of the report it is based on – which we cannot endorse."[27]

---

23. ABC News, 29 December 2008.
  www.abc.net.au/news/2008-12-29/hamas-to-blame-for-provoking-israel-gillard/251888.
24. Patricia Karvelas, "Rudd Defends Israel's Rights", *The Australian*, 6 January 2009.
25. Sarah Smiles and Kate Laherty, "Turnbull Supports Israeli Response", *The Age*, 5 January 2009.
26. UN General Assembly 2009.
27. Quoted in A. Shapiro, "Australia opposes Goldstone Report", *Australian Jewish News*, 13 November 2009.
  https://www.aph.gov.au/About_Parliament/Parliamentary_Departments/Parliamentary_Library/pubs/BN/2012-2013/AustraliaIsraeliPalestinianConflict#_ftn44.

During the 2014 assault on Gaza, the Liberal prime minister Tony Abbott employed the classic deflection that avoids any question about Israel's culpability and blames Palestinians. In an interview on radio 3AW he said:

> Well, we certainly support Israel's right to exist. We support Israel's right to self-defence and we deplore the attacks on Israel from Gaza. Now I don't have any further detail on what may or may not be happening at the moment. All I know is that Israel is regularly rocketed from Gaza.[28]

The Abbott government swung the pendulum even further in Israel's direction. It refused to call East Jerusalem "occupied" and withdrew support for a UN resolution urging a halt to the construction of settlements in occupied territories.

Abbott continued to campaign for Israel from the backbench. In 2017 he called for all aid to be cut from Australia to the Palestinian Authority, a move that was subsequently enacted. After Donald Trump announced that the US embassy would be moved to Jerusalem from Tel Aviv, a declaration that was provocative in the extreme, Abbott urged the Australian government to do the same.[29] For his fierce loyalty to Israel, Abbott was awarded an honorary doctorate in Israel in 2017.

Malcolm Turnbull did not deviate in substance from the Liberals' positioning under Abbott. He warmly hosted Netanyahu when he visited Australia and condemned both the UN and those who "insisted government take the side of those in the international community who seek to chastise Israel – and it alone – for the continuing failure of the peace process".[30]

This brief history illustrates an increasingly close relationship between Israel and Australia, prompted by a variety of shifts and

---

28. Interview with Tony Abbott, 18 July 2014.
   http://pmtranscripts.pmc.gov.au/release/transcript-23652.
29. Fergus Hunter, "Tony Abbott calls for Palestinian aid cut and embassy relocation to Jerusalem", *Sydney Morning Herald*, 2 January 2017.
   https://www.smh.com.au/politics/federal/tony-abbott-calls-for-palestinian-aid-cut-and-embassy-relocation-to-jerusalem-20170102-gtkk4d.html.
30. Latika Burke, "Malcolm Turnbull affirms Israel support, criticises UN, ahead of Benjamin Netanyahu visit", *Sydney Morning Herald*, 22 February 2017.

changes in the Middle East since the 1960s – shifts that have made Israel a bedrock of Western power in the region.

Trade

One argument sometimes advanced for the close relations between Australia and Israel is the importance of trade relations. Although this is emphasised by both governments, the actual levels of trade could in no way justify the level of support given to Israel. While there has been some recent growth, Israel's trade with Australia has been a minor proportion of total trade for both countries. It has always been dwarfed by Australia's extensive trade, primarily in wheat, sheep, meat and minerals, with various Arab states. Australia is Israel's 22nd principal export destination. Australia is 38th on the list of Israel's import sources. Israeli-Australian trade is worth $88 million a year.

Australia and Israel have regularly signed agreements related to trade and joint research and development. There has also been discussion of further cooperation in communications, agricultural technology and water management, biotechnology and defence. This trade has been facilitated by the Australia-Israel Chamber of Commerce, which says this of itself on its website:

> The Australia-Israel Chamber of Commerce (AICC) is Australia's preeminent international Chamber of Commerce and one of the country's most prestigious and active national business organisations. The AICC's national membership exceeds 1,000 leading Australian companies across a broad range of industry sectors. Fifteen of the top 25 companies in Australia are currently members or sponsors of the AICC.[31]

Despite the relatively small size of the trade relationship, the political connections are significant. Every year the Australia-Israel Chamber of Commerce runs trade missions to Israel. The "mission leaders" for these trips are drawn from Australia's top politicians. This kind of overlap between the political and the economic hints at the basis for the bilateral commitment. It suggests that the intimacy is based

---

31. Australia-Israel Chamber of Commerce. http://www.aicc.org.au/pages.cfm?id=24.

more on the military and political role that Israel can play in the region, rather than economics. The geostrategic imperative is vital. An added factor is that the Israeli economy is intertwined with its military. Marxist economist Adam Hanieh notes the crossover in personnel between the military and bureaucracy on one hand, and corporate executives on the other:

> As Israel's economy has undergone transformation...the new capitalist class emerged from the fusion of indigenous private capital linked to the state, foreign (mainly US) capital buying into state-owned enterprises, and former state bureaucrats and military officers who had led the privatisation process. In this latter regard more than 75 percent of the key executive personnel of Israel's top 100 private companies come from high ranking positions in the Israeli state bureaucracy, while Israel's corporate boardrooms boast significant numbers with high ranking military experience.[32]

Such connections mean that Australia's political ties to Israeli bureaucracy and military can easily extend to closer economic relations than one might expect from the volume of trade alone. These realities hint at the importance of Israel's imperial, military and political role in the region as the basis for the backing of both the US and Australia, rather than a simple trade relationship.

The myth of a "moral" Australian state

Another rationale for the unprecedented level of Australian support for the Israeli state has been the "moral imperative". Evidence reveals a contrary dynamic: a hard-headed, cynical attitude to both the Jewish population in Australia and to the migration to Australia of Jews from trouble zones. The warmth or hostility toward Australian Jews on the part of the ruling class can be understood only in relation to two factors: their integration into and commitment to Australian capitalism, and the imperialist needs of the ruling class at any given time. In the early colonial period, the Jewish population was relatively integrated into Australian society. Historian Hilary

---

32. Hanieh 2003.

Rubenstein describes the colonial era as the "golden age of Jewish participation in the political life of Australia".[33]

After 1840, Jewish congregations were to be found in many country towns even though only two country synagogues now survive. Up to the beginning of the gold rush of the 1850s, British Jews made up 90 percent of the Australian Jewish population. Although this numerical predominance was later lost, it set the tone for Australian Jewry until the 1930s and "created an Anglo-Jewish atmosphere of orthodoxy and efficiency, piety and dignity, modernity of method with strict adherence to tradition".[34] This demographic factor had political consequences. Many historians note the political conservatism of this early Jewish population and its tendencies to identify as staunchly British and pro-imperialist. While some sections of the ruling class exhibited anti-Semitic prejudices, this didn't stop prominent Jews from becoming part of the establishment. Two governors-general of this period were Jewish. To the extent that ruling-class Jews were in agreement with the imperial interests of Britain (and therefore Australia), they were welcomed.

Increasing turmoil and anti-Semitic agitation in the 1920s and 1930s drove Yiddish-speaking Eastern European Jews to Australia in large numbers. The response from the Australian state and the Anglophile Jewish population was hostile. Both feared the political and social disruption that a non-English-speaking Jewish population might bring. As violent anti-Semitism rose across Europe, the government placed strict limitations on refugees. The Minister for Trade and Customs, the aptly named Thomas White, claimed at a conference in 1938 that while the government had admitted some German and Austrian Jews, in the circumstances Australia could do no more. "Australia was not desirous of importing a racial problem by encouraging any scheme of large-scale foreign migration."[35]

Limitations were placed on Jews coming into Australia on the ships commandeered by the International Refugee Organisation.

---
33. Rubenstein 1987, p25.
34. Crown1987.
35. Reich 1995, p187.

They placed so-called "Jewish clauses" on these refugees, making a distinction between Jews from Europe's east and west. If Jewish immigrants were to come, those from the latter area were preferred because they were considered to be more easily assimilated. Sir Samuel Cohen, foundation president of the Australian Jewish Welfare Society, argued for even stricter limitations in July 1939: "Our council is in favour of even more vigorous handpicking than the government in its wisdom and kindness has seen fit to impose."[36]

This push to curb Jewish migration occurred during the pogroms against European Jews and continued despite mounting evidence of the horrors of the Holocaust. It seems the moral conscience of the Australian ruling class was absent without leave – or more likely with leave. And official hostility towards increased Jewish migration dovetailed with Australia's eventual support for the establishment of Israel. It gave the government an argument for denying entry to refugees.

The myth of the Zionist lobby

There is a widespread belief that a Zionist lobby with unusual strength operates in Canberra and is the overwhelming reason for Australia's historic commitment to Israel. Such an assertion cannot be sustained historically. Zionism as a political ideology was a minority current among Australian Jews until the eve of the establishment of Israel. Most historians of Australian Zionism acknowledge the difficulty Zionist organisations had getting off the ground in the nineteenth and early twentieth centuries. A survey taken in 1908 indicated that there were 20 different Zionist societies in Australia, but many of them were small and short-lived.[37]

The Jewish National Fund, whose files on Australia begin in 1912, reveals the efforts made by the World Zionist Organisation to create interest in Australia by sending frequent emissaries. The

---
36. Rubenstein 1987, p32.
37. Central Zionist Archives, letter dated 7 February 1908, from A. Nesbit to the Central Zionist office in Berlin, cited in Rubenstein 1987, p32.

first was Israel Cohen, from the London office, who, during his visit in 1921, noted:

> The devotion of the [Melbourne] Jews to the British Crown is sincere and ever present, and struck me as much more demonstrative in character than that of their co-religionists in the mother country. So fond were they of singing the national Anthem at the gatherings in which I appeared that I was almost inclined to think that they regarded me not so much as an Emissary of the Zionist Executive, as an Envoy of His Majesty.[38]

Zionist membership was marked by shekel sales. In 1921, 100 shekels were sold in Sydney, 200 in 1922 and the same number in 1923. In Perth, 93 shekels were sold in 1922 and 500 in 1923. In Melbourne, 1,500 shekels were sold in 1923. These sales were small and proportionate to the Jewish population of the time.

The Zionist movement was also not uniformly committed to establishing a Jewish state in Palestine. There were territorialists who were for establishing a Jewish community in Australia. One of the leading proponents of these schemes was Israel Zangwill, who made plans to buy one million acres of land in the outback for the settlement of 500 to 1,000 families. These schemes were dismissed without hesitation by state and federal governments, which were extremely unwilling to allow the establishment of a "state within a state". Even when international Zionist campaigning increased in the 1930s, many Anglo-Australian Jews remained aloof. They felt that to support Israel would call their Britishness into question. The Zionist terrorist bombing of British targets in Palestine was widely condemned by the Jewish press in Australia. While a minority of Jews (mainly those more recently arrived from Eastern Europe) were serious Zionist campaigners, establishment figures were lukewarm. Zionist emissary Shimon Hacohen wrote home to Jerusalem in 1946:

> A big part of the community of this city are [sic] opposing us almost openly. This comes from two angles; the left-wing and the right-wing anglicized Jews...in Melbourne where such persons as a

---

38. Cohen 1968, p128.

leading Rabbi and Sir Isaac Isaacs are openly coming out on the platform against us.[39]

It was only after the British had left Palestine and the state of Israel was a *fait accompli* that Anglo-Australian Jews began to feel comfortable with Zionism. As Ralph Sander, a Sydney youth leader, found in 1949: "Because 'Zionist' is no longer a synonym for 'Anti-British' many barriers have been lifted".[40]

This history reveals the fallacy of the notion of a strong, cohered, cashed-up Zionist lobby that through its weight pressured the government into support for the establishment of Israel. To make this point is not, however, to deny that there were prominent Zionist figures who did have the ear of key establishment figures. Evatt was clearly impacted by some of these individuals, and they contributed to Australian policy-making. Nevertheless, the lobby argument doesn't hold water given the low level of Zionist organising prior to 1948. Zionism and support for Israel were a minority current in the Australian Jewish population until the very eve of the establishment of Israel.

The situation today is the polar opposite: Zionism is the dominant ideology among Australian Jews. In a 2009 survey of Australia's Jewish population, 80 percent of respondents indicated that they regarded themselves as Zionist, while only 13 percent did not. When asked for their reaction to international events which put Israel in danger, a large majority indicated that they felt a "special alarm" (56 percent) or as if their own life was in danger (20 percent).[41] Professor Fania Oz Salzberger made the following comment, indicating how dramatically support for Israel has developed over the last 60 years:

> I am yet to find a single Australian Jew who is indifferent towards Israel. There is a level of proximity here that one cannot find amid British or American Jewry, where many individuals are unstirred by their

---

39. Rabbi John Simon Levi, "Doubts and fears: Zionism and Rabbi Jacob Danglow", in Rubenstein 1987, p162.
40. ibid, p12.
41. Markus et al 2009.

Jewish ancestry, uninvolved with Israel, or both. I like telling my Jewish Australian friends that they are first cousins to us Israelis, while many other communities are second cousins at best.[42]

This transformation is the outcome of the convergence of the needs of Australian capitalism with the consolidation and strengthening of the Israeli state. In the last 60 years, powerful institutions and organisations have developed that push a pro-Israel agenda in almost all spheres of Australian cultural, political and economic life. These include the Australia Israel and Jewish Affairs Council (AIJAC), the Zionist Federation of Australia (ZFA), Australian Union of Jewish Students (AUJS), the Australia-Israel Chamber of Commerce (AICC) and many others. These organisations dominate political life in the Jewish community and attempt to create a cultural environment that is extremely pro-Israel. Probably the most powerful of these, the AIJAC, describes its role: "Through research, commentary, analysis and advocacy, AIJAC represents the interests of the Australian Jewish community to government, politicians, media and other community groups and organisations."[43]

Jewish interests are almost completely conflated with Israeli interests in all of these organisations. The activities of the Australian Union of Jewish Students illustrate the point. One of the major AUJS campaigns for 2013 was entitled "My Israel". It had a website devoted to the campaign, which featured a series of posters of Israeli citizens celebrating Israel and lauding its inclusiveness. One of these was clearly responding to the well-documented racism towards African refugees in Israel.[44] It stated:

> My Israel is the fulfilment of the dream of my ancestors in Ethiopia to immigrate to Israel. This is the undisputed home of a beautiful, versatile and unique democratic Jewish lifestyle. It is respect for equality and

---

42. Fania Oz Salzberger, "Who's afraid of the Israeli Left?", *Australian Jewish News*, 5 June 2009.
43. Australia Israel and Jewish Affairs Council, http://aijac.org.au/about-aijac/.
44. Toi Staff, "52% of Israeli Jews agree: African migrants are 'a cancer'", *Times of Israel*, 7 June 2012.
    http://www.timesofisrael.com/most-israeli-jews-agree-africans-are-a-cancer/.

freedom for all citizens of different religions as well. Israel is my home, my family, my roots, the essence of caring for each other.[45]

This is part of the AUJS attempt to project a positive image of Israel on campus and to hegemonise the debate around Israel/Palestine. Here, not only is AUJS associating Jewishness with Israel, it is also waging an argument that any critique of Israel is anti-Jewish. This is a more general trend. AIJAC, the ZFA, AUJS and AICC all intervene aggressively to clamp down on criticism of Israel. Many of them focus particularly on media depictions of Israel. Antony Loewenstein described this campaign in his book, *My Israel Question*:

> In October 2003 AIJAC released a report alleging systematic bias at SBS news and current affairs in relation to the Israel-Palestine conflict… It also objects to SBS calling the West Bank, Gaza and East Jerusalem "occupied Palestinian land". Why? According to the report, "It is indisputably the case that this land has never previously been under the sovereignty of either the Palestinian people or a state called Palestine, nor is there any legally binding UN decision or international treaty that says it should be."… I submitted a freedom of information request to SBS requesting all documentation related to Middle East programs between 2001 and 2003. I eventually received a bundle of documents that confirmed my suspicions: the vast majority of 29 letters of complaint submitted to SBS news and current affairs management about Middle East coverage were from AIJAC's Colin Rubenstein or other AIJAC staff, and all fit a similar pattern.[46]

Further examples abound. In 2012 the Executive Council of Australian Jewry (ECAJ) submitted a 20-page letter of complaint to the SBS ombudsman about the drama *The Promise*. *The Promise* details the experiences of British soldiers at the end of the mandate and a young British woman visiting Palestine and Israel for the first time in the 2000s. The ECAJ opposed its screening in the most strident terms. They maintained that the depiction of Jewish terrorism (both against the British and in well-documented events like the massacre of Palestinians in the village of Deir Yassin) was

---

45. Cited at https://www.jwire.com.au/aujs-up-and-running/.
46. Loewenstein 2009, p192.

akin to Nazi propaganda and was reflective of a rehabilitation of anti-Semitism.[47] The conflation of any critical look at Israel's history with anti-Semitism is widely used against critics of Israel. SBS denied the charges and went on to sell the DVD of the program.

More recently, Zionist groups attempted to curtail the expression of critical views in the media by Loewenstein. In early 2013 the ABC broke the mysterious story of Ben Zygier, an Australian man found dead in an Israeli prison. As it turned out, Zygier was a Mossad spy who had gone rogue and landed in jail. The story prompted an avalanche of public discussion about the actions of Mossad and the relationship of Australian Jews to Israel. In response, the ABC radio program *AM* ran an interview with Loewenstein in which he called for public discussion about "the relationship between the Jewish establishment in Australia and the Israeli government, and indeed Mossad, and indeed Israeli intelligence and the Israeli embassy".[48] This was enough to provoke a full-frontal attack from the ECAJ, which issued a complaint and a press release stating its objection to the public airing of Loewenstein's views. According to ECAJ executive director Peter Wertheim, the ABC had launched a baseless attack on Australian Jews, with insinuations of disloyalty, by interviewing someone whom the ABC itself describes as a "provocateur". Upon review, the ABC found that it had done nothing to contravene its anti-discrimination policy. The virulence and frequency of such complaints by the ECAJ and other organisations illustrates the determination of Zionist organisations to quash public debate about Israel.

The hysterical response by *The Australian* to a motion passed by the Greens-influenced Marrickville Council in 2011 is another case in point. When the council decided to boycott particular Israeli goods, all hell broke loose. *The Australian* and the *Sydney Morning Herald* waged an almost daily campaign of slander and invective

---

[47]. Joshua Levi, "TV series 'The Promise' akin to Nazi propaganda", *Australian Jewish News*, 13 January 2012.
[48]. "Zygier case wake up call for Jewish community", *AM*, ABC radio. http://www.abc.net.au/am/content/2013/s3691806.htm.

against the Greens. Accusations of anti-Semitism abounded. This press campaign was aimed at creating an environment in which public support for Palestine was seen as unacceptable. In the end, the council backed down, and the Greens watered down their support for the Boycott, Divestment and Sanctions campaign at their national conference.[49] Heresies (like support for Palestinian human rights) were hunted. Political sacrifices were made. The pro-Zionist barrage had its intended effect. Public debate was quashed and pro-Palestine sentiment was vilified.

One of the major programs designed to help frame political opinions about Israel is run by AIJAC. It is the Rambam Israel Fellowship program, which annually sponsors visits to Israel. At a recent event celebrating 10 years of this program, guests heard that AIJAC had sent more than 400 politicians and journalists, together with political advisers, senior public servants and student leaders. Included among the alumni are Prime Minister Julia Gillard and Opposition Leader Tony Abbott.[50] These are propaganda trips, designed to show off Israeli virtue and to sanitise the occupation of the West Bank. The participants don't go to Gaza and see the rubble or meet maimed and traumatised Palestinians. Rather they meet politicians from the Palestinian Authority who more often than not are in collaboration with the Israeli war machine. These sponsored programs obviously play a role in strengthening Australian politicians' commitment to Israel, but they are not the whole story. Groups like AIJAC promote a global agenda that fits neatly with Australian imperialism. The home page of its website lists "Islamic extremism" as one of the main issues with which it concerns itself.[51]

AIJAC whipped up Islamophobia to justify the US-led invasions of Afghanistan and Iraq and the threat Islamism supposedly poses within Australia and other Western societies. "The growth of Islamic extremism in Asia also constitutes an important issue

---

49. Amos Aikman and Leo Shanahan, "Greens forced to back down on Israel boycott", *The Australian*, 20 April 2011.
50. Henry Benjamin, "Rambam 10 Years Old", *J Wire*, 3 September 2012. https://www.jwire.com.au/rambam-10-years-old/.
51. http://aijac.org.au/about-aijac/.

not only for all Australians, but Israel and the Australian Jewish community in particular."[52]

In a context where the Australian ruling class strongly backed the invasions of Afghanistan and Iraq and also uses the threat of Islamic extremism to further its regional agenda against Indonesia, organisations like AIJAC can play a very useful role for them. The conflation of Arab with "terrorist", a core component of pro-Israel propaganda, is connected fundamentally to the global imperial agenda of the Australian ruling class.

Conclusion

Empathy for the plight of European Jewry or special cultural affinity was not the motivating force for the Australian ruling class to back Israel in 1948. The ongoing intimacy between the two states is not based on the same plucky determination to defy authority. Nor is it due to Australia simply trotting along behind the US like an obedient puppy. Australia backs Israel because doing so fits with Australian capitalism's material and geopolitical interests in the Middle East and across the world. There is nothing reluctant about the Australian state's current backing of Israel. Geopolitical interests are bolstered by a series of significantly sized and economically powerful organisations that could be termed a Zionist lobby. This lobby bullies, corrals, persuades and provides political arguments for the Australian state's support for Israel. But Australia's support for Israel does not emerge from the lobby.

---

52. ibid., accessed 27 February 2013
(archived at https://web.archive.org/web/20130227203741/http://www.aijac.org.au/about-aijac/).

CHAPTER SIX

Palestinian Resistance

> The fish,
> Even in the fisherman's net,
> Still carries,
> The smell of the sea.
>   - Mourid Barghouti[1]

The Arab word *sumud* is often used to describe the Palestinian struggle. It means "steadfast" and refers to the seemingly unbreakable determination of the Palestinian people to survive and resist. From the earliest period of Zionist colonisation Palestinians rioted, struck and protested. Such resistance has inspired other struggles across the region and the world. Indeed, one of the most iconic images of resistance in the twentieth century comes from Palestine: a young man with a rock in hand, facing down the impervious strength of an Israeli tank. This is an image of unparalleled bravery and it rightly continues to inspire.

The history of Palestinian resistance is, however, much more than a tale of bravery against all odds. Like any other resistance movement, the Palestinian struggle has, from the earliest days, been riven with debates about what liberation means and how it should

---

1. Barghouti 2005.

be fought for and won. Despite the popular romantic vision, which, like any nationalism, mythologises a unified Palestinian identity, there have always been social, economic and political divisions within the Palestinian population. These divisions have extended into the resistance and prompted important debates. Which political organisations end up winning these debates has been a key factor in shaping Palestinian politics and therefore the lived realities for millions of Palestinians. This chapter will offer both a breakdown of the class dynamics in Palestine over the decades and brief histories of some of the most significant Palestinian resistance organisations. It will then give a detailed account of the two Intifadas (or rebellions) and conclude with the most recent developments around the Arab Spring and after. Woven through this history is an argument about the necessity of a strategy for Palestinian liberation that involves regional working-class revolution.

Class dynamics in early Palestine

The area known as Palestine has always had a rich and chequered history. It was fought over by the Babylonians, the Assyrians, the Egyptians, the Romans, the early Muslims, and the Crusaders. By the early modern period, however, Palestine was dominated by the Ottoman empire and ruled by networks of tribal clans. The detail of such history is beyond the scope of this modest pamphlet but it is important to note that Palestine was a "patchwork quilt of different cultures, religions and ways of life spawned by endless waves of invasion... [This produced] an anarchic bonhomie where Maghribi mystics, Armenian craftsmen, Talmudic scholars, British mercenaries, Turkish gendarmerie and Greek Orthodox traders lived side by side with the merchants, landowners and religious elite who made up the upper echelons of Sunni Muslim society".[2]

By the late nineteenth century Palestinian society was ruled by a small number of landowning families who had inherited large

---
2. Smith 1984, p8.

landed estates, and another set of wealthy families who could be characterised as an intellectual, religious aristocracy. This period saw a rapid decline in subsistence farming and a rise in cash crops and production for export, particularly hard wheat, olives and citrus fruit. As the Ottoman empire declined, various European powers smelled blood and began to circle. They gained control over huge sections of economic activity including banking, transport and communications, public utilities and mining. Additionally, a series of measures was implemented right across the failing areas of the Ottoman empire and parts of Europe encouraging immigration to the region. These early migrants included Jewish agricultural settlers. By 1900 around 500 such migrants had arrived. These dynamics led to increased land speculation, with the rich and powerful from across the Arab world buying up tracts of land. Large areas of Palestine were now owned by absentee landlords. Class differentiation in the countryside grew apace, with an extremely wealthy landowning class exploiting and dominating a rural working class, landless tenants, sharecroppers and impoverished small farmers. The small but rapidly developing rural working class was made up of locals who had been thrown off their land by the rich Arab landowners and were forced to scrounge for work.

Over this period, cities began to develop and with these, new layers of urban merchants and artisans and craftsmen. Nevertheless, the first post-war census in 1922 put the portion of those living in the countryside at 81 percent. These class dynamics would be very important for the politics of Palestinian resistance in the period leading up to the establishment of the British mandate. The breakdown of old social traditions prompted turmoil. Some peasants and the rural proletariat clung to old ways, myths and religions, while others found new forms of political expression. The First World War saw outbreaks of struggle and a flourishing of ideas. Between 1908 and 1914, Palestinian newspapers such as *Al-Karmel* and *Filastin* campaigned against political Zionism – advocating a nationalist response to increasing Jewish settlement – and against the British mandate. There is evidence that these papers sold well in working-class suburbs and workplaces.³

As we have seen, the interwar period saw an increase in Zionist migration coupled with a more aggressive British occupation, all of which prompted resistance. By the mid- to late 1930s many of these tensions reached boiling point and they exploded in the revolt of 1936. Every town, city and village had some form of organisation supporting the strike. Arab shops, businesses and markets closed down. Civil disobedience reigned across the country, as Palestinians refused to pay taxes, occupied public buildings and organised street demonstrations. Transport and communication ground to a halt. In the countryside, small bands of guerrillas swelled in number and by the end of the revolt it was estimated that there were 5,000 Palestinians under arms. The British high commissioner described the country as being in an "incipient state of revolution", with "little security or control of lawless elements outside principle towns, main roads and railways".⁴

The revolt was a genuine cross-class mobilisation. The main slogan of the revolt was "Independence for Palestine!" and the dominant politics was Palestinian nationalism. While in some places, like Jaffa, Palestinian workers played a key role, in others their action was limited by their small numbers and the increasing strength of the Jewish working class. In Haifa for instance, the most significant industrial city in Palestine, Palestinian port workers were sacked en masse and replaced with Jewish labour. Workers, while taking specifically working-class action to achieve their national demands, were unable to form a significant separate organisation. This proved to be a major impediment to extending the strike beyond the limited objectives of the middle class and the old landowning class. Such a failure of organisation and leadership proved fatal in places like Haifa, where many Arab business owners, terrified of defeat and frustrated with the disruption the strike was

---

3. Beška 2014, p55.
4. Marshall 1989, p62.

causing to their profits, cut deals with the British and the Zionists and worked with them to undermine the strike.

Ultimately the general strike was defeated both by British repression and the political inadequacies of the Palestinian resistance. Here the failures of the Palestine Communist Party, an organisation that purported to hold internationalist revolutionary politics, became clear.

The Palestine Communist Party

Of the organisations that had an orientation to the working class, the Palestine Communist Party (PCP) was one of the most significant. Initially, when the PCP was formed in 1923, it was dominated by leftist Jews who had moved to Palestine as part of the Labour Zionist movement. This population was deeply influenced by the Russian Revolution and committed to building a revolutionary working-class movement. They were hostile both to the British mandate and also to what they saw as a ruling-class Zionist movement. While they were not hostile to Arabs, they had no base in the local Palestinian population. Chronicler of the PCP Musa Budeiri argues that "The Communist movement in Palestine was born within the confines of the Zionist movement in complete isolation from the Arab inhabitants of the country".[5]

The focus of the activists who would go on to become the initial core of the PCP was initially on organising working-class Jews in the Yishuv (Zionist enclaves). This orientation was challenged after 1924, when the PCP applied to join the Communist International. The Comintern strongly encouraged the PCP to turn toward organising Arab workers by relating to their struggles against the British mandate and the attempts by the Zionists to dominate all industry and push out Palestinian workers. Indeed, the PCP now threw itself into heroic battles against what was known as the Zionist "conquest of work".[6] They even organised armed pickets of both Jews and

---

5. Buderi 2010, cited in Michael Fiorentino, "Palestine's left before Israel", *International Socialist Review*, 80, November 2011.
6. An attempt by Zionist employers to enact apartheid policies in the workplace by

Arabs to target Zionist bosses who were sacking Palestinian workers. As a result, despite a difficult start, the PCP managed to organise a party that had both Arab and Jewish members. Such an attempt at revolutionary internationalism was both brave and necessary, but it was riven with tensions.

The fate of the PCP was not merely decided, however, by events in Palestine. One of the most decisive factors was the developing situation in the USSR. A counter-revolution led by Stalin oversaw the destruction of the genuine revolutionary traditions of 1917. Stalin developed a highly centralised state-capitalist regime that desired to become a major player on the global stage. For the Stalinist USSR, the Comintern became a body through which the interests of the Russian ruling class could be pursued internationally. The various communist parties became subject to the dictates of the USSR. The twists and turns of Russian foreign policy were reflected in the positions taken by communist parties across the world. The PCP was no different.

In 1935 the Stalinist regime decided to enter into more conciliatory relationships with the West. The corollary of this turn was what came to be known as the Popular Front. Rather than emphasising class war, the Comintern embraced cross-class alliances. In situations of national oppression this policy was particularly disastrous. At worst it meant opposing self-determination altogether, which became the CP's attitude in Vietnam and Algeria, and at best it meant uncritically embracing bourgeois nationalism and downgrading the importance of independent working-class organisation. In Palestine, the Popular Front manifested in a policy of opening the door to supposedly progressive, middle-class elements in both the Jewish and Arab camps. The PCP now emphasised the righteousness of the nationalist aspirations of both Jews and Arabs. Instead of espousing working-class internationalism, both Jews and Arabs were now to fight for their own national state. Such a position increasingly led to divisions between the Arab and Jewish members of the party.

---

only employing Jewish workers.

These tensions were amplified during the 1936 Palestinian revolt. While showing solidarity with the anti-colonial struggle, the PCP was increasingly sublimating its politics both to Arab nationalism and the notion of a Jewish nationalism.

Further divisions opened up during the Second World War. Initially the PCP was hostile to the war, which sat well with its anti-British campaigning. But once the USSR joined the Allies, the PCP swung behind the war effort and even encouraged its members to join the British army. This led to a split, with many Arab members leaving to form the National Liberation League (NLL). The PCP was left with a marginal rump with no real commitment to international working-class revolution.

When the state of Israel was declared in 1948, the USSR was one of the first countries to recognise it. The PCP members who still understood Israel as a colonial project were thrown into disarray. Such a stance saw them lose any remaining support among Palestinians, and although they clung on organisationally for decades, they ended up being largely irrelevant to the shaping of Palestinian resistance politics for the rest of the twentieth and twenty-first centuries.

Arab nationalism

The period after World War Two saw the rapid growth of Arab nationalism. As nationalist regimes came to power in Egypt, Syria and Iraq, they became the receptacle of the hopes of millions. Enthusiasm for Arab nationalism spanned all classes. The poor felt that the expulsion of the Western colonial powers would inevitably lift their living standards; the middle classes, frustrated by the lack of opportunity for intellectual development and career advancement, hoped that the nationalist regimes would provide them with new paths; while the rich desired the abolition of colonial limitations over their wealth and power. In large part, the nationalist regimes focused on fulfilling the hopes of the latter two classes. Nevertheless, the seeming defiance and radical rhetoric of the regimes held broad appeal; the initial economic success of Nasser in Egypt and the

Ba'athists in Iraq and Syria prompted a great wave of nationalism. Slogans calling for Arab unity in opposition to imperialism and (Western-style) capitalism were chanted across the region. These developments shaped the Palestinian movement.

After the Nakba, Palestinians were scattered across the region and became part of local political movements. Jabber, Lesch and Quant argue that many Palestinians (particularly students) found themselves associated with the Muslim Brotherhood, others with the Syrian Social Nationalist Party (SSNP), still others with the Arab Socialist Ba'ath Party or the Arab Nationalist Movement (ANM). Many were attracted to the leadership of Egypt's president Gamal Abdel Nasser, especially after 1956, while others accepted positions within the Jordanian establishment.[7] This led many moderate Palestinian activists, such as those who formed Fatah, into close relationships with various Arab regimes.

Radical Palestinian nationalists were more sceptical of the Arab regimes but held a romantic conception of Arab unity. National divisions in the Arab world were, they argued, the creation of colonialism. A strong Arab movement across national boundaries could challenge both the imperialists and the Zionists, and they argued that the liberation of Palestine would come with the development of a strong pan-Arab nation. Hopes on this front rose between 1958 and 1961, when Egypt and Syria formed the United Arab Republic (UAR). In 1961 after a power struggle, the Syrians left the union and in practical terms the possibility of a pan-Arab superstate diminished. The bulk of the enthusiasm remained, however, with the Egyptian regime. The closeness of the relationship between the Palestinian movement and the regimes across the region has been one of the key fault lines in Palestinian politics for decades. Time and again, it has undermined the capacity for an independent, truly revolutionary Palestinian movement to develop.

The main Arab nationalist organisation in which Palestinians were prominent was the Arab Nationalist Movement. It was led by

---

7. Jabber et al 1973, p49.

the Christian Palestinian George Habash and embodied much of the radical nationalist sentiment of the era. Its slogan was "Unity, Freedom, Revenge, Blood, Steel, Fire".[8] After 1967 however, the movement was in decline, and the subsequent crisis led many in the ANM towards versions of "Marxism-Leninism".

The PLO and Fatah

After the Arab defeat in the war with Israel in June 1967, many Palestinians felt let down by the Arab regimes. Wider layers began to feel that their own liberation would not be achieved by following meekly behind the Arab regimes. A new path must be forged. There was an uptick in an independent Palestinian nationalism; doctrines of self-reliance began to dominate. In carving out a clearer and more determined resistance they felt they could cohere a significant movement, both of the Arab masses and, importantly, the Arab states, behind them.

A slew of new commando and political groups were established and a new iteration of Palestinian nationalism began to flourish. The mid- to late 1960s saw the coalescing of some of the most significant Palestinian organisations for the coming decades: Fatah, the Popular Front for the Liberation of Palestine (PFLP), the Democratic Front for the Liberation of Palestine (DFLP) and the main umbrella organisation of the Palestinian national movement, the Palestine Liberation Organisation (PLO).

The PLO was established in 1964 by leaders of the Arab regimes who wanted a Palestinian movement they could control, but by 1969 the Palestinian Resistance Movement (or Fatah) had taken over its leadership and began to transform it in its own image.

Fatah began its life in the Palestinian diaspora in Kuwait, Egypt, Jordan and the Gulf States in 1958. Its leadership developed out of the disenfranchised middle classes and some of the big Palestinian capitalists. Yasser Arafat, who led Fatah for over 20 years, was a civil engineer who came to own a number of large engineering companies

---
8. Marshall 1989, p112.

in the region. Much of Fatah's funding came from Palestinian bankers and merchants whose wealth survived the 1948 establishment of Israel because it was already invested abroad. On the other hand, much of Fatah's rank and file were ex-peasants or the urban poor who comprised the bulk of the refugee-camp Palestinians.

The frustration of those living in refugee camps and the radical zeitgeist of the late 1960s initially led Fatah to adopt a series of radical nationalist positions. They argued for the liberation of all of historic Palestine (from the Jordan River to the Mediterranean Sea) and refused to recognise Israel as a legitimate state. They also demanded the right of return for all those refugees expelled in the 1948 war. Nevertheless, the political dominance of the Palestinian bourgeoisie clearly influenced Fatah's political program and tactics. The organisation's goal was to establish a Palestinian capitalist state that its members could control and rule, with their own working class to exploit. Fatah therefore never encouraged working-class or broader revolutionary social struggle; its leaders feared this kind of activity would get out of control and threaten their own class position.

Instead they focused on mobilising a mass guerrilla army under the slogan of revolutionary violence. They established camps where *fedayeen* (fighters) were trained. Prior to 1970 these camps were overwhelmingly in Jordan. From here Fatah launched a series of high-profile actions designed to capture territory that Fatah leaders could then declare an autonomous Palestinian zone. One of the most dramatic of these actions occurred in the East Bank town of Karameh in 1968, when they claimed the first Arab victory over the Israeli military. Support for Fatah grew rapidly.

While initially the Jordanian regime had tolerated the existence of the *fedayeen*, the growth of an increasingly popular and uncontrollable force within their borders was of grave concern to the Hashemite monarchy. By 1970, Fatah and the PLO had gained such authority among Palestinians within Jordan that King Hussein declared them a "state within a state". They controlled many of the camps, provided welfare, established parallel civic administrations and controlled one section of the Jordanian border. There was also increasing sentiment among a poorer, more radical section of the Palestinian camp populations that it was necessary to overthrow the Jordanian regime. The Fatah leadership was, however, wary of such arguments. Much of their orientation was to draw the Arab regimes (including the Jordanian one) into direct confrontation with Israel, thereby broadening the forces that would be arrayed against the Zionists. Fatah leader Khalid al-Hassan explained the strategy:

> We intended to provoke and capture the imagination of the Palestinian and Arab masses. We thought we could create a new atmosphere in which no Arab leader would dare to ignore the subject of liberating Palestine... [W]hen the Arab leaders were coming under pressure for action from their own masses, we would engage them in dialogue. We would ask them to join us in planning a coordinated strategy for the actual liberation of our homeland.[9]

They did not recognise the thousand threads that tied the Jordanian regime to capitalist stability and the imperial order. Any head-on confrontation with Israel or the US would threaten its own power and privilege.

In September of 1970 however, Fatah was forced into backing a general strike demanding democratic representation of Palestinians in the Jordanian state. Given that 70 percent of the Jordanian population was Palestinian, the regime's odds of maintaining control in such a situation were small. It moved swiftly against Fatah and the PLO, and with the backing of the US and Israel mobilised a crushing military offensive. Over the course of the next year thousands of Palestinians were murdered, and Fatah's base of operation was completely dismantled. This whole disastrous affair became known as Black September and revealed in no uncertain terms where, when the chips were down, the Arab regimes would line up.

While publicly Fatah was forced to take a critical stand toward the Jordanian regime, it didn't drop its general policy of non-interference

---

9. ibid., p117.

towards other Arab leaders and regimes. It shifted its base of operation to Lebanon, and mounted a strident case that the best way to avoid another Black September was to develop friendlier relations with other regimes and to be more careful about its operations. This desire to appease the capitalist Arab regimes was reflective of the whole cross-class approach of Fatah and the PLO. If your desire is simply to establish a Palestinian state that could eventually become part of Middle East power plays, then you have to prove your capacity to acquiesce to the capitalist status quo.

By the late 1970s Fatah declared that the liberation of all Palestine was off the agenda for the foreseeable future. By the 1980s Arafat suggested that the movement should limit its demands to a Palestinian mini-state in the Occupied Territories – the two-state solution. At first this was presented as a temporary measure, an immediate demand that, once achieved, would place the movement in a better position to fight for full liberation. But this was a historic capitulation, as it abandoned the idea of a democratic, non-sectarian state in the whole of historic Palestine. Increasingly, the PLO dropped its emphasis on armed struggle and shifted toward negotiations. This trajectory was halted somewhat when the Intifada of 1987 exploded many of the certainties of the Palestinian political situation up to this point.

Intifada

Palestinian resistance had been centred among the diaspora. The Intifada saw the populations of Gaza and the occupied territories of the West Bank take centre stage.[10] On 8 December 1987 four workers from Gaza were killed by the Israeli military at a checkpoint. This prompted a wave of strikes and demonstrations, followed by a violent crackdown by Israeli forces. At the height of the Intifada, Israel had more than 175,000 troops deployed to suppress the protests.

Mobilisations continued into 1988 and much like in 1936, local

---

10. In Arabic, *intifada* means to rise up or shake off.

committees were established in every area. The youth of Palestine came to the fore, displaying verve, energy and zeal. The iconic images of Palestinian struggle come from this Intifada; of young people, heads covered by keffiyehs, hurling stones from slingshots at the Israeli military. A people unbroken and unbowed. They rediscovered the tactics from the earlier period: refusal to pay taxes, the closure of shops, boycotts of Israeli products and mass street demonstrations. Confidence rose among the Palestinian population and much of the action was led by independent forces.

Palestinian workers began to strike against Israeli bosses. A January 1988 communiqué from the Unified National Leadership of the Uprising captures some of the dynamic – increased working-class confidence but expressed in nationalist terms:

> To the Palestinian working class: Yes, the arms of steel have succeeded through their participation in the strike in stopping the machines in thousands of Israeli factories and workshops. Your role in this uprising is unique and special. Continue your strike against work in Israeli factories, oh heroic workers. We will not be frightened by frantic threats uttered by the Zionist authorities, courts and employers, for in this uprising we have nothing to lose but our chains and the oppression and exploitation befalling us. Let us paralyse the machine of Israeli production because enhancing the Israeli economic crisis is one of our weapons on the road to achieving our right to return, to self-determination, and to establish an independent national state.[11]

Unfortunately, while Palestinian workers did begin to mobilise as workers, they were in a strategically weak position. The Israeli economy did not rely predominantly on Palestinian labour. Unlike the apartheid regime in South Africa, where the state and economy were utterly dependent on oppressed black workers, the Israeli state had created a separate economy. So while the withdrawal of Palestinian labour certainly disrupted some sectors of the Israeli economy, workers' action could not deal a knockout blow. This was to become an important factor in undermining the strength of the Intifada.

---

11. Hiltermann 1991, p178.

Despite the huge levels of bravery, resistance and almost unprecedented levels of social mobilisation inside Palestine, the Intifada did not manage to free Palestine. Here the question of political leadership again came to the fore. While there was a series of political organisations that had a following (the PFLP, the DFLP, Islamic Jihad and the PCP) the dominant force in the Intifada became, yet again, Fatah. Throughout the 1980s Fatah had continued to dominate the PLO and sideline other political forces, but regaining control over the situation at the beginning of the Intifada proved a challenge. The PLO's image had been tarnished by previous failed ventures and the perception among sections of the Palestinian population that it was out of touch with life in the Occupied Territories. Nevertheless, the PLO managed to employ radical nationalist rhetoric and gain popular support, all the while steering the movement into acceptable channels.

Phil Marshall summarises the outcome:

> As the Uprising continued, Arafat used his new-found strength once again to rally the Arab states behind the mini-state strategy. Thus Fatah directed the movement in characteristic fashion: although the Uprising had given the PLO greater freedom from the influence of the Arab states, Arafat used his room for manoeuvre to orient the organisation back toward the Arab regimes.[12]

Furthermore, the disruption of the Intifada had prompted the Israeli state to reassess its strategy. Direct occupation seemed less feasible than before. Much better to find a willing Palestinian partner: a force that could control the Palestinian population better than Israel could. As Prime Minister Yitzhak Rabin explained in an interview with the Israeli newspaper Yediot Aharonot:

> I prefer the Palestinians to cope with the problem of enforcing order in Gaza. The Palestinians will be better at it than we were because they will allow no appeals to the Supreme Court and will prevent the [Israeli] Association for Civil Rights from criticizing the conditions there. They will rule there by their own methods, freeing – and this

---

12. Marshall 1989, p161.

is the most important – the Israeli Army soldiers from having to do what they will do.[13]

Israel managed to find a more than willing partner in Arafat and Fatah.

The Fronts

The abject capitulation of the forces of Fatah prompts the question: what of the revolutionary Marxist left? Unfortunately the history of the two main organisations that called themselves revolutionary, the Popular Front for the Liberation of Palestine (PFLP) and the Democratic Front for the Liberation of Palestine (DFLP), was extremely chequered.

The PFLP was established by the radical nationalist George Habash in 1967, and a few years later Nayef Hawatmeh and Yasser Abd Rabbo led a leftist split to form the DFLP. Both organisations were influenced by a Maoist-inflected radical nationalism and this seriously limited their potential. They used the language of class struggle but, like many Third Worldist movements such as the NLF in Vietnam, they did not consider the working class as the agent of liberation. In their theoretical writings and organisational practices they emphasised the struggle of the "oppressed masses". Habash in particular used this populist language of Maoism to provide a theoretical underpinning to the organisation. They put particular emphasis on guerrilla organisation and established a series of training camps across the region, using these committed activists to launch a series of high-profile plane hijackings. Such terrorist activity came to replace an emphasis on building popular working-class support in Palestine, among the diaspora and beyond.

In their early phase the Fronts developed an important critique of Fatah's orientation to the Arab regimes. They maintained that the regimes were too tied into world imperialism to be trustworthy allies in the struggle for a liberated Palestine. Such a position was sorely needed. Over time, however, this position changed. The PFLP for instance increasingly made a distinction between the

---
13. Blanford 2011.

reactionary Arab regimes and the supposedly progressive ones. This led the PFLP to develop ties to the dictatorial Assad regime in Syria and the Ba'athist government in Iraq. Furthermore, the PFLP throughout the 1970s increasingly enlisted backing from the USSR and China. Over time this had a marked effect on its political positioning. It became uncritical of the regimes associated with the USSR and China and thus subordinated itself to the global imperial rivalry between the various powers.

The DFLP was initially very critical of the PFLP's line on these questions, but quickly shifted sharply to the right. It eventually took the dubious honour of being the first champion of the so-called two-state solution.

Though the PFLP never made such a terrible concession on paper, in practice it has settled in to being a loyal opposition within the corrupted and compromised structures of the PLO.

The Second Intifada

Despite these political limitations, the Palestinian resistance was not over. The Second Intifada erupted in 2000 after Israel's right-wing defence minister Ariel Sharon stormed into one of the most important holy sites for Palestinians, the Al-Aqsa Mosque in East Jerusalem. Sharon entered the compound surrounded by more than 1,000 armed troops in a move that was designed as an extreme provocation, an assertion of untrammelled Israeli power. The move backfired when riots, demonstrations and protests broke out across the Occupied Territories. Within days these protests had escalated dramatically and a full-scale conflict ensued.

The scale of the Second Intifada was similar to the first in terms of its breadth and initial popular involvement, but there were some significant differences. The Oslo years had left their legacy. The people of Gaza and the West Bank were frustrated and bitter, having had their expectations of a peace dividend raised, then crushed. The Palestinian Authority held onto power but was not popular. In reality the uprising was against the horrific living conditions imposed by both Israel and the PA. Ramzy Baroud, Palestinian writer and a participant in the Second Intifada, argues: "It is only human, following decades of disproportionately dispensed suffering, violence and dispossession that one's determination to attain freedom would partly concede to an overpowering sense of desperation and raw desire for vengeance".[14]

Despite the fact that Fatah was the dominant force inside the PA and the PA was increasingly unpopular, the Fatah-dominated PA still maintained a certain level of control over the key institutions of the uprising. Nevertheless, their star was waning. Into the breach stepped a number of Islamic organisations – Islamic Jihad and Hamas being the two most prominent. It is important to note that during the Intifada all these organisations operated alongside each other. Hamas and IJ both acknowledged the leadership of Fatah and made no move to openly undermine the PA's control.

The Second Intifada was significantly more militarised on both sides. While initially the impulse among Palestinians living in the Occupied Territories was toward mass mobilisation, the levels of desperation, combined with a political leadership more oriented to an armed response, militarised the struggle. Guerrilla groups grew in size and authority. This meant that the Second Intifada was much bloodier than the first. In the first six weeks of the uprising, Israeli forces killed more than 200 Palestinians and injured almost 8,000.

The uprising continued until Israel withdrew from the Gaza strip in 2005.

Hamas

Hamas's origins lie in the Palestinian Muslim Brotherhood, which was established in 1946. It was a branch of the Egyptian Muslim Brotherhood, a bourgeois Islamic organisation with branches across the Middle East. Up until the first Intifada in 1987, the Palestinian Muslim Brotherhood abstained from the resistance movement, concentrating instead on Islamic consciousness-raising and doing

---

14. Cited in Tenne 2007.

"good works" in the community. Because of this abstentionism and its conservative social agenda, the Brotherhood was the preferred organisation of Israel and the US.

The beginning of the first Intifada, however, saw a marked shift in the organisation's emphasis. Its leadership began to recognise that it would be marginalised if they abstained from the struggle. Thus the Islamic Resistance Organisation (or, using the Arabic acronym, Hamas, which also means "Zeal" in Arabic) was established in 1987.

During the first Intifada, Hamas threw itself into the struggle and began to grow in size and influence. Their combination of Islamic teaching, charity work and determined resistance gained them popularity, but it was the failure of Oslo in the 1990s and the increasingly obvious corruption of the Fatah leaders that brought Hamas to the centre stage of Palestinian political life.

This culminated in 2006, when Hamas won control of the Palestinian Legislative Council. This election represented a historic shift in Palestinian politics, away from the dominance of Fatah and the PLO. This was not welcomed by Western imperialism and Israel, which had been fostering and funding Fatah as their loyal servant in the Palestinian movement. Israel, with the backing of most of the "civilised" world, immediately launched an all-out offensive against Hamas, including the assassination of many of its leaders and the devastating blockade of basic goods and services to Gaza.

During this time Hamas put itself firmly in the tradition of both political Islamism and Palestinian national liberation. Its leaders drew on the values of Islam while also situating themselves as the inheritors of the genuine liberation movement. Yet despite their declarations that they are different from Fatah, the similarities were and remain manifold. Hamas's leadership is primarily drawn from middle-class elements within the Occupied Territories: clerics, ex-doctors and lawyers, and also full-time party officials living away from Palestine. Its cadres consist of merchants, businesspeople and the rich as well as the middle class, while the poor remain largely a passive base of support.

Outside of Palestine, rich Muslim businesspeople in the Gulf countries represent the main source of Hamas funding. Because of this social base, Hamas tends to sympathise with the goals of the Palestinian bourgeoisie. Like Fatah, Hamas believes in the necessity of an alliance between all classes in Palestinian society. In practice, this means that the interests of the Palestinian refugees and workers must be subordinated to those of the Palestinian capitalists.

Because of this Hamas does not hold a principled, democratic hostility towards the ruling classes of the Arab regimes: regimes which are well practised in the oppression and exploitation of their own working people. Indeed, Hamas seeks the approval and funding of some of the most right-wing Islamic monarchies in the region, such as Iran.

So in many ways Hamas's attitude mirrors Fatah's position of non-interference in the affairs of Arab countries. Hamas cannot orient to the working masses of the Arab world as allies in the movement for the liberation of Palestine, as the masses have a serious interest in overthrowing their own hated regimes: regimes which Hamas wants to align itself with.

Ultimately its desire for an independent Palestinian capitalism leaves Hamas on shaky ground when it comes to genuine liberation for the Palestinian masses. Hamas does not reject capitalism; it does not reject the exploitative and competitive class relationships that lie at the heart of imperialism. Indeed, Hamas has never rejected "free enterprise", subscribing to the belief within the circles of the Islamist movements that Islam encourages trade and entrepreneurial activities. On economic policy Hamas tends to accept the pro-market ideas pushed by the US and its financial arms, the IMF and the World Bank. What's more, the fact that Hamas looks to regimes like Iran with admiration – regimes where free and independent trade unions are banned and where militant workers are tortured and killed – suggests something about its attitude to the working class and its organisations.

The truth of the matter is that Hamas does not want to unleash working-class forces across the region that might threaten not only the Arab regimes, but also the potential economic base of a future Palestinian capitalism. So for instance, while it put out limited calls for action during the initial uprising in Egypt in 2011, when the Muslim Brotherhood took dictatorial control, Hamas shut up.

Hamas's desire to establish a Palestinian capitalism also means that it cannot take a consistent stand against US imperialism and is subject to the same internal dynamics that pushed Fatah in the direction of compromise. That sections of the Hamas leadership have considered recognising Israel in exchange for minor concessions indicates a similar trajectory. So while it is the case that Hamas grew in popularity because of its willingness to fight the Israeli state and its refusal to accept the continuing degradation of Palestinian life, there is nothing in its politics or social composition that would allow it to take a fundamentally different road from Fatah.

The Arab Revolutions

In 2011 the politics of the region were transformed by the explosion of what was widely known as Arab Spring. Beginning in Tunisia, with Egypt soon to follow, dictators were overthrown as millions of workers and the oppressed hit the squares and the streets, went on strike, burned down police stations and stormed government buildings. The revolutions were the product of a cauldron of simmering economic and political tensions, and decades of authoritarian neoliberalism. The Middle East looked like it was being born anew. All the old certainties, all the old borders and boundaries, all the longstanding enmities and sectarian divisions were thrown into disarray.

In the centre of the revolt in Cairo, Tahrir Square, the creativity of the masses was unleashed in the early days of the revolution. Protesters not only took over the square, but organised food distribution, security, political education and cultural entertainment. In other parts of Egypt, strikes halted industry. In other parts of the country, centres of political power were besieged. One Egyptian protester, Ahmad Mahmoud, captured the mood of the times: "When we stopped being afraid we knew we would win."[15]

The Arab revolutions and Palestine

The question of Palestine had long been of import to the Arab masses. The dispossession and ongoing oppression of the Palestinians held deep symbolic power; their suffering was Arab suffering writ large. Furthermore, the brave and seemingly uncompromising struggle of the Palestinians, despite all the odds, has fired the spirits and imaginations of millions across the region. Almost every period of upheaval in Palestine was complemented by mass protests in the Arab world.[16] These protests were not simply protests of solidarity. In many cases, in Morocco, Syria and Jordan and beyond, the mobilisations evolved from merely expressing sympathy with the Palestinian cause to anti-government protests in their own right. In this way it has become clear to many that their own ruling classes presided over the maintenance of a system that oppressed the Palestinians and committed their own populations to poverty and political repression.

The Arab Spring expressed many of these dynamics. Firstly, because of the historic interconnection of the Arab world, the revolutions were international in scope. The rebellions across the region raised expectations in Palestine. Ahmad Abu Arab expressed a common sentiment. "For 63 years we've been under occupation," he said. "Everywhere else in the world people are finding their freedom, but not the Palestinians. Now is our time."

On 15 May 2011, 50,000 Palestinian refugees from the camps in the south of Lebanon descended on the village of Maroun er Ras near the Lebanese-Israeli border. A journalist described the scene:

> With the narrow winding road leading to Maroun er Ras blocked by parked buses, entire families – from toddlers to stooped and wrinkled old men – began climbing the steep northern slopes of the hill to reach the

---
15. David McNally, "Transformed by the revolution", *Socialist Worker* (US), 15 February 2011. https://socialistworker.org/2011/02/15/transformed-by-revolution.
16. Bloodworth 2007.

village. Colourfully dressed Palestinians steadily walked up the verdant flower-speckled hillside in narrow winding columns, red, green and black Palestinian flags fluttering in the spring breeze.[17]

Thousands of these protesters charged the border fences, and with the rage of years pushed with all their strength. At this point the Israeli and Lebanese military began firing directly into the crowd, using live bullets. Ten Palestinians were killed.

Syria saw equally as dramatic scenes. Palestinian refugees – old, young, men and women – marched to the border. Snaking in their thousands down the hill to the barbed wire separating them from their homeland, the protesters, in direct reference to the Arab revolutions, chanted *"Al-Sha'b yureed tahreer falasteen"* (The people want the liberation of Palestine). They then climbed the fence, and after rocking back and forth for some moments, managed to pull it down. The marchers were then joyfully greeted by Palestinians living on the Israeli-occupied side, and in breathless, beautiful scenes, they mingled, embracing each other. As tears flowed, one man was heard to say "This is how liberation is."

For a brief period, it looked like the Arab Spring might blossom in Palestine. This was not to be. Not only did the Israeli state maintain a tight grip on the Occupied Territories and Gaza, but the Palestinian political leadership refused to answer the call. The Palestinian Authority failed to organise mass mobilisations in the Occupied Territories. Their events were small and symbolic. In Gaza, Hamas similarly ducked the opportunity. While Egyptian revolutionaries were marching on the border zone near Gaza, Hamas steadfastly refused to mobilise Gazans en masse to greet them. Independent forces were too small and lacking in confidence to organise around these "resistance" behemoths. Why? What can account for such a gross, determined refusal to grasp the opportunities offered by the Arab Spring? Unfortunately, the political leaderships of the Palestinian movement had, by 2011, become so entrenched within the networks of power and privilege, so constrained by their

---

17. Blanford 2011.

relationships with other regimes and so fearful of unleashing the power of mass action, that they considered the maintenance of their existing patch of power more important than utilising the opportunity presented to them to overturn the status quo.

More broadly, it became clear by the end of 2011 that the capitalist order across the Middle East was fighting back. In Egypt, the deep state stepped out of the dark with General al Sisi at its head. In Bahrain the Saudis helped the regime behead the movement, murdering activists and freedom fighters in their thousands. In Tunisia, large sections of the movement were co-opted and the struggle channelled into the safe waters of parliamentary debate. In Syria the Assad regime sought to drown the mass revolutionary movement in nerve gas and mortar fire. Whole cities like Aleppo have been turned into rubble, and millions have been displaced and turned into refugees. From this counter-revolution, forces like ISIS have emerged who want to destroy the old borders in the name of the creation of a new pan-Islamic state. New reactionary political forces have sprung up and formerly radical currents have been tested and failed.[18]

While the promises of the initial phase of the Arab Spring have not been fulfilled, the period demonstrated a few vital lessons. Firstly, the struggles across the Middle East are deeply international. Mobilisations in one part of the region quickly spill into others. The ruling class of the region understands this and this is why they have been so determined to squash rebellion; either through co-option and a pretence of concern for Palestinians or through bloody repression. The internationalism of movements from below is important. The Israeli state is one of the strongest in the region, indeed the world. It is a nuclear power and is backed by the largest military force in the world, the USA. Israel is also a significant economic power that is connected through a thousand threads to the other economies in the region. The Palestinians,

---

18. It is beyond the purview of this chapter to discuss these dynamics but for more detail see Bloodworth 2011.

by contrast, are a small population with very little real economic power. Workers in Palestine, if they withhold their labour, do not have the capacity to completely cripple the Israeli economy. But international workers' rebellion across the Middle East can cripple the networks of capital that dominate the region.

Similarly, the military struggles of the Palestinians are completely outgunned and outmanned by Israel. This isn't to say that these struggles aren't important, but it is to point out that on their own, the odds are stacked against them. The disparity in power is one of the reasons that many in the Palestinian movement have turned to "realistic solutions" such as negotiations with imperial forces such as the EU or the USA, or pleading with the stronger Arab regimes to come to their aid. "Realism" in the Palestinian struggle becomes merely another word for unforgivable concessions. Arab ruling classes have always and will always be more interested in regional power and privilege than solidarity with the Palestinian poor. The prospect of a future Palestinian state offers no economic or political carrots to sway the ruling classes of the EU or USA to disrupt their very comfortable relationship with Israel and other regional powers. The struggles of the masses in 2011 demonstrated magnificent levels of courage. But for these kinds of struggles to be successful they require more than just determination and bravery. They require a clear and independent revolutionary politics.

The Palestinian struggle, as this chapter has demonstrated, has been plagued by many political pitfalls, Stalinism and variants of class-collaborationist nationalism being the two most dominant. The trajectories of the Communist Party, Fatah, the Fronts and now Hamas have demonstrated the dead end of nationalism, whether in traditional, Stalinist or Islamist forms. What is needed is a new, refreshed revolutionary movement. One that refuses to accept the status quo of regional power. One that refuses to deal in the politics of compromise and collaboration. One that centres on the rights and desires of the poor, the oppressed and workers and does not desire a Palestinian capitalist mini-state. The struggle for Palestine has the capacity to be a struggle for much more. For Palestinian workers and the poor, freedom means more than the freedom to be exploited by a more powerful Palestinian capitalist. A free Palestine should mean a Palestine free of exploitation and oppression. A Palestine truly worthy of the many heroic lives sacrificed for it.

References

Abunimah, Ali 2011, "Interview: Alice Walker on the Gaza Freedom Flotilla and the struggle for justice", Electronic Intifada, 17 June. https://electronicintifada.net/content/interview-alice-walker-gaza-freedom-flotilla-and-struggle-justice/10090

Alsaafin, Linah 2011, "Are the Freedom Rides a detour for the struggle?", Electronic Intifada, 23 November. https://electronicintifada.net/content/are-freedom-rides-detour-struggle/10616

Amnesty International UK 2017, Gaza: Operation Cast Lead, 16 February. https://www.amnesty.org.uk/gaza-operation-cast-lead

Aruri, Naseer 2002, "Oslo: Cover for territorial conquest", in Lance Selfa (ed.), The Struggle for Palestine, Haymarket Books, Chicago.

Ayoub, Dr Hasan S., 2016, Settler violence: An armed wing of settlement expansion in the occupied Palestinian territory, Premiere Urgence Internationale (PUI) and Médecins du Monde – France (MDM). https://www.premiere-urgence.org/wp-content/uploads/2016/06/rapport-palestine-english-v3.pdf

Barghouti, Mourid 2005, I saw Ramallah, Bloomsbury Publishing, London.

Barr, James 2011, A Line in the Sand: Britain, France and the struggle that shaped the Middle East, Simon and Schuster, London.

Barrows-Friedman, Nora 2011, "Archbishop Desmond Tutu endorses 'Freedom for Palestine' song," Electronic Intifada, 21 June. https://electronicintifada.net/blogs/nora-barrows-friedman/archbishop-desmond-tutu-endorses-freedom-palestine-song

Beinin, Joel 1990, Was the red flag flying there? Marxist politics & the Arab-Israeli conflict in Egypt and Israel, 1948-1965, Tauris, London.

Beinin, Joel 1999, "The demise of the Oslo process", Middle East Report Online, 26 March. https://merip.org/1999/03/the-demise-of-the-oslo-process/

Bell, Coral 1993, A dependent ally: a study in Australian foreign policy, Allen and Unwin, St Leonards, NSW.

Beška, Emanuel 2014, "Political opposition to zionism in Palestine and Greater Syria: 1910–1911 as a turning point", Jerusalem Quarterly, 59 (Summer), January. https://www.researchgate.net/publication/270282548_Political_Opposition_to_Zionism_in_Palestine_and_Greater_Syria_1910-1911_as_a_Turning_Point

Blanford, Nicholas 2011, "Palestinian refugees call for third intifada during deadly clashes at Israel Lebanon border", Christian Science Monitor, 15 May. https://www.csmonitor.com/World/Middle-East/2011/0515/Palestinian-refugees-call-for-third-intifada-during-deadly-clashes-at-Israel-Lebanon-border

Bloodworth, Sandra 2007, Nationalism and the Arab revolutions, Socialist Alternative, Melbourne.

Bloodworth, Sandra 2011, "Marxism and the Arab revolutions", Marxist Left Review, 2, Autumn. https://marxistleftreview.org/articles/marxism-and-the-arab-revolutions/

Borochov, Ber Dov 1906, Polaei Tziyon: our platform. https://www.jewishvirtuallibrary.org/quot-poalei-tziyon-our-platform-quot-ber-dov-borochov

Buderi, Musa 2010, The Palestine Communist Party, 1919-1948: Arab and Jew in the struggle for internationalism, Haymarket Books, Chicago.

Burns, Ailsa 2010, "Why Australia supports Israel", New Matilda, 9 March. http://newmatilda.com/2010/03/09/why-australia-supports-israel

Chomsky, Noam 1999, Fateful triangle: the United States, Israel, and the Palestinians, South End Press, Cambridge Massachusetts.

Cockburn Andrew and Leslie Cockburn 1991, Dangerous liaison: the inside story of the U.S.-Israeli covert relationships, Harper Collins Publishers, New York.

Cohen, Israel 1968, The journal of a Jewish traveller (1925), cited in P.Y. Medding, From Assimilation to Group Survival: a political and sociological study of an Australian Jewish community, F.W. Cheshire.

Crown, Alan D. 1987, "Demography, politics and love of Zion: The Australian Jewish community and the Yishuv, 1850-1948", in W.D. Rubenstein (ed.), Jews in the Sixth Continent, Allen & Unwin, Sydney.

Embassy of Israel in Australia [n.d], "Bilateral relations: a historical overview", http://embassies.gov.il/canberra/Relations/Pages/Bilateral-Treaties-and-Agreements.aspx

European Union 2019, Six-month report on Israeli settlements in the occupied West Bank, including East Jerusalem, January-June. https://eeas.europa.eu/delegations/palestine-occupied-palestinian-territory-west-bank-and-gaza-strip/68152/node/68152_tm

Finkelstein, Norman 2018, "Palestinians have the right to break free of the 'unlivable' cage that is Gaza,", Democracy Now, 16 May. https://www.democracynow.org/2018/5/16/norman_finkelstein_palestinians_have_the_right

Robert Fisk 1992, Pity the nation: Lebanon at war, Oxford University Press, Oxford.

Gasper, Phil 2002, "Israel: colonial settler state", in Lance Selfa (ed.), The Struggle for Palestine, Haymarket Books, Chicago.

Gitelman, Zvi 2003, "A century of Jewish politics in eastern europe: the legacy of the Bund and the Zionist movement", in Zvi Gitelman (ed.), The Emergence Of Modern Jewish Politics: Bundism And Zionism In Eastern Europe, University of Pittsburgh Press.

Haddad, Toufic 2009, "The road to Gaza's killing fields", International Socialist Review, 64, March. https://isreview.org/issue/64/road-gazas-killing-fields

Hammer, Julianne 2009, Palestinians born in exile: diaspora and the search for a homeland, University of Texas Press, Texas.

Hanieh, Adam 2003, "From state-led growth to globalisation: the evolution of Israeli capitalism", Journal of Palestinian Studies, 32 (4), Summer. https://jps.ucpress.edu/content/32/4/5

Hanieh, Adam 2013, "The Oslo illusion", Jacobin, 21 April. https://www.jacobinmag.com/2013/04/the-oslo-illusion/

Harman, Chris 2006, "Hizbollah and the war Israel lost", International Socialism, 2:112, Autumn. http://isj.org.uk/hizbollah-and-the-war-israel-lost/

Harris, Marty 2012, "Australia and the Middle East conflict: a history of key government statements (1947-2007)", 13 August, http://www.aph.gov.au/About_Parliament/Parliamentary_Departments/Parliamentary_Library/pubs/BN/2012-2013/AustraliaMiddleEastConflict#_Toc332632588

Hiltermann, Joost R. 1991, Behind the Intifada, Princeton University Press.

Tikva Honig-Parnass and Toufic Haddad (eds) 2007, "Introduction" in between the lines: readings on Israel, the Palestinians and the US war on terror, Haymarket Books, Chicago.

Jabber, Faud, Ann Mosley Lesch and William Quandt 1973, The politics of Palestinian nationalism, University of California Press.

Kanafani, Ghassan 1999, Men in the sun and other Palestinian stories, translated by Hilary Kilpatrick, Lynne Rienner Publishers Inc., London.

Kaplan, Fred 2006, "There are worse things than the status quo", Slate, 24 July, https://slate.com/news-and-politics/2006/07/condi-s-witless-optimism-about-the-middle-east.html

Leon, Abram 1950, The Jewish question: a Marxist interpretation. https://www.marxists.org/subject/jewish/leon/index.htm

Loewenstein, Antony 2009, My Israel question, Melbourne University Press.

Loewenstein, Antony 2011, "Is Australia capable of

showing any backing for Palestine?", 8 August. https://antonyloewenstein.com/is-australia-capable-of-showing-any-backing-for-palestine/

Levi, Rabbi John Simon 1987, "Doubts and fears: zionism and Rabbi Jacob Danglow", in W.D. Rubenstein (ed.), Jews in the Sixth Continent, Allen and Unwin, Sydney.

Marfleet, Phil 2015, "An end to isolation? Palestine and the Arab revolutions", International Socialism, 2:145, Winter. https://isj.org.uk/an-end-to-isolation-palestine-and-the-arab-revolutions/

Markus, Andrew, Nicky Jacobs and Tanya Aranov 2009, Report series on the Gen08 Survey. "Preliminary findings: Melbourne and Sydney", Australian Centre for Jewish Civilisation, Monash University. https://www.jca.org.au/wp-content/uploads/2017/06/Gen08-Preliminary-Findings.pdf

Marsden, Chris 2003, "Opposition to US Middle East 'road map' escalates", World Socialist Website, 11 June. https://www.wsws.org/en/articles/2003/06/mide-j11.html

Marshall, Phil 1989, Intifada: zionism, Imperialism and Palestinian resistance, Bookmarks, London.

Newsinger, John 2006, The blood never dried: a people's history of the British Empire, Bookmarks, London.

Pappé, Ilan 2004, A history of modern Palestine: one land, two peoples, Cambridge University Press, Cambridge.

Pappé, Ilan 2006, "The 1948 ethnic cleansing of Palestine", Journal of Palestine Studies, 36 (1), pp6-20. www.jstor.org/stable/10.1525/jps.2006.36.1.6

Pappé, Ilan 2008, The ethnic cleansing of Palestine, One World, London.

Piggot, Leanne 2008, Australia and Israel: a pictorial history. https://www.dfat.gov.au/sites/default/files/pictorial_history.pdf

Poole, Steve 2006, Unspeak: how words become weapons, how weapons become a message, and how that message becomes reality, Grove Press, New York

Quince, Anabelle 2016, Drawing a line in the sand: 100 years of the Sykes-Picot Agreement, 19 May, https://www.abc.net.au/radionational/programs/rearvision/100-years-of-the-sykes-picot-agreement/7423030

Reich, Chanan 1995, "Australia and the Jewish community of Palestine: 1915-1941", in Peter Y. Medding, Studies in Contemporary Jewry, XI: Values, Interests, and Identity: Jews and Politics in a Changing World, Oxford University Press, New York.

Reich, Chanan 2002, Australia and Israel: an ambiguous relationship, Melbourne University Press, Melbourne.

Rose, John 1986, Israel, the hijack state: America's watchdog in the Middle East, Bookmarks, London.

Rose, John 2004, The myths of zionism, Pluto Press, London.

Rubenstein, Colin 2008, "Australia and Israel: a unique friendship", The Drum, 13 March. https://www.abc.net.au/news/2008-03-13/37466

Rubenstein, Colin and Tzvi Fleischer 2007, "A distant affinity: the history of Australian-Israeli relations",Jewish Political Studies Review,19:3-4,14November.https://jcpa.org/article/a-distant-affinity-the-history-of-australian-israeli-relations-2/

Rubenstein, Hilary 1987, "Jewish non-distinctiveness to group invisibility: Australian Jewish identity and responses, 1830-1950", in W.D. Rubenstein (ed.), Jews in the Sixth Continent, Allen and Unwin, Sydney.

Said, Edward, 2003 "A road map to where?," London Review of Books, 25 (12), 19 June. https://www.lrb.co.uk/the-paper/v25/n12/edward-said/a-road-map-to-where

Smith, Ashley 2018, "Illiberal hegemony: the Trump administration strategy for US imperialism", International Socialist Review, 109, Summer. https://isreview.org/issue/109/illiberal-hegemony-trump-administration-strategy-us-imperialism

Smith, Pamela Ann 1984, Palestine and the Palestinians 1876 to 1983, St Martin's Press, New York.

Suarez, Thomas 2017, State of terror: how terrorism created modern Israel, Olive Branch Press, Northampton.

Tenne, Ruth 2007, "Rising of the oppressed: the second Intifada", International Socialism, 2:116, Autumn. http://isj.org.uk/rising-of-the-oppressed-the-second-intifada/

United Nations General Assembly 2009, A/RES/64/10, follow-up to the "Report of the United Nations fact-finding mission on the Gaza conflict", 5 November. Archived at https://web.archive.org/web/20140812212133/http://www.un.org:80/News/Press/docs/2009/ga10883.doc.htm

United Nations 2018, Office for the Coordination of Humanitarian Affairs Press Release, "2018: more casualties and food insecurity, less funding for humanitarian aid". https://www.un.org/unispal/document/2018-more-casualties-and-food-insecurity-less-funding-for-humanitarian-aid-ocha-press-release/

The World Bank, Gaza and the West Bank, 1 October 2019. https://www.worldbank.org/en/country/westbankandgaza/overview

This work was published by Red Flag Books, an imprint of the revolutionary organisation Socialist Alternative.

Red Flag Books offers hundreds of other titles covering Marxist politics, revolutionary history, and more.

Browse our store at *shop.redflag.org.au*

—

Read on to discover other important projects that help to equip us with the ideas we need to fight back and win against capitalism.

Spreading the revolutionary ideas we need for a world in crisis.

REDFLAG

The newspaper of Socialist Alternative

Australia's #1 socialist publication relies on your support to continue. Read now and subscribe.

redflag.org.au

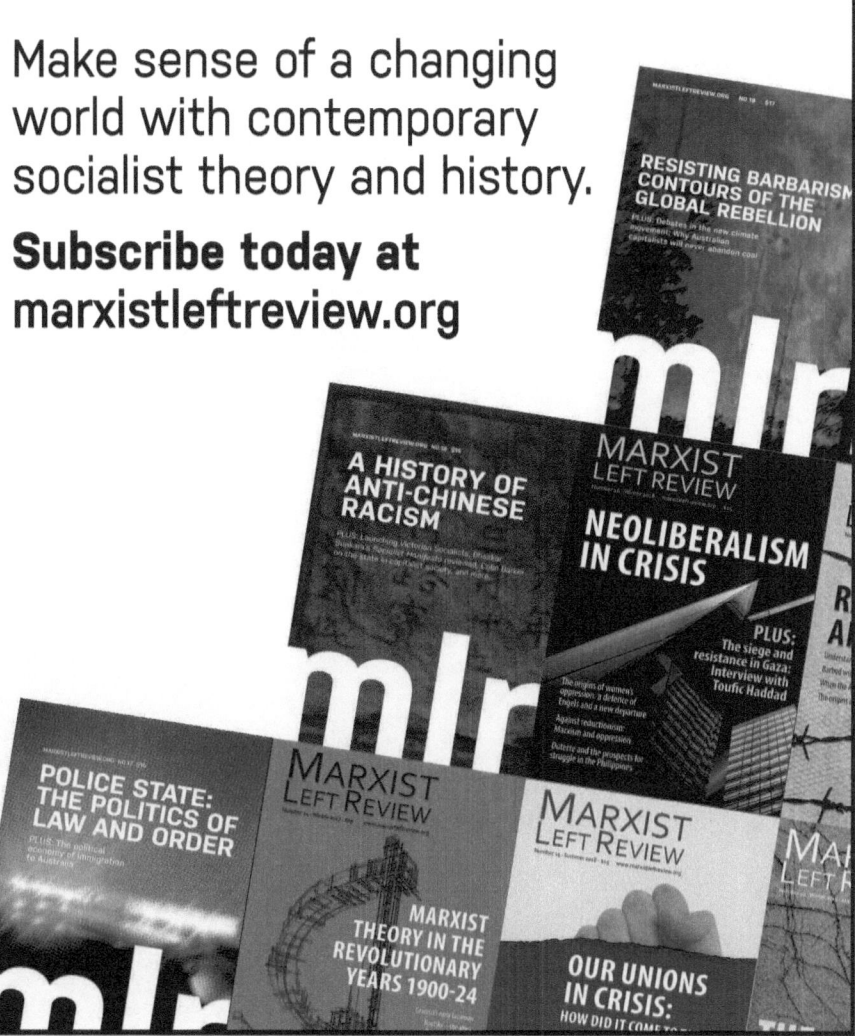

www.ingramcontent.com/pod-product-compliance
Lightning Source LLC
Chambersburg PA
CBHW032044290426
44110CB00012B/944